Natural Man, Citizen, Philosopher

THE McDONALD
CENTER FOR
AMERICA'S FOUNDING
PRINCIPLES

MERCER
UNIVERSITY

THE A. V. ELLIOTT CONFERENCE SERIES

Guided by James Madison's maxim that "a well-instructed people alone can be permanently a free people," the McDonald Center exists to promote the study of the great texts and ideas that have shaped our regime and fostered liberal learning.

Will R. Jordan and Charlotte C. S. Thomas, Directors

No Greater Monster nor Miracle than Myself: The Political Philosophy of Michel de Montaigne, ed. Charlotte C. S. Thomas (2014)

Of Sympathy and Selfishness: The Moral and Political Philosophy of Adam Smith, ed. Charlotte C. S. Thomas (2015)

The Most Sacred Freedom: Religious Liberty in the History of Philosophy and America's Founding, ed. Will Jordan and Charlotte C. S. Thomas (2016)

Promise and Peril: Republics and Republicanism in the History of Political Philosophy, ed. Will R. Jordan (2017)

When in the Course of Human Events: 1776 at Home, Abroad, and in American Memory, ed. Will R. Jordan (2018)

Power and the People: Thucydides' History and the American Founding, ed. Charlotte C. S. Thomas (2019)

From Reflection and Choice: The Political Philosophy of the Federalist Papers and the Ratification Debate, ed. Will R. Jordan (2020)

Liberty, Democracy, and the Temptations to Tyranny in the Dialogues of Plato, ed. Charlotte C. S. Thomas (2021)

The Beginning of Liberalism: Rexamining the Political Philosophy of John Locke, ed. Will R. Jordan (2022)

The Founding: Essential Documents, ed., Will R. Jordan (2023)

Governing Oneself and Others: On Xenophon of Athens, ed. Charlotte C. S. Thomas (2024)

Natural Man, Citizen, Philosopher

The Political Philosophy of
Jean-Jacques Rousseau

Edited by Will R. Jordan

MERCER UNIVERSITY PRESS
Macon, Georgia

Endowed by
TOM WATSON BROWN
and
THE WATSON-BROWN FOUNDATION, INC.

MUP/ P714

Published by Mercer University Press
1501 Mercer University Drive
Macon, Georgia 31207

29 28 27 26 25 5 4 3 2 1

Books published by Mercer University Press are printed on acid-free paper that meets the requirements of the American National Standard for Information Sciences—Permanence of Paper for Printed Library Materials.

Printed and bound in the United States.

This book is set in Adobe Caslon.

Cover/jacket design by Burt&Burt.

ISBN 978-0-88146-962-2

Cataloging-in-Publication Data is available
from the Library of Congress

CONTENTS

CONTRIBUTORS

LAURENCE D. COOPER—Professor of Political Science, Carleton College, Northfield, Minnesota

CHRISTINE DUNN HENDERSON—Associate Professor of Political Science, Singapore Management University, Singapore

WILL R. JORDAN—Professor of Political Science, Co-Director of the McDonald Center for America's Founding Principles, Mercer University, Macon, Georgia

CHRISTOPHER KELLY—Professor of Political Science, Emeritus, Boston College, Chestnut Hill, Massachusetts

EMMA PLANINC—Assistant Professor of Political Science, University of Notre Dame, South Bend, Indiana

DENISE SCHAEFFER—Professor of Political Science, College of the Holy Cross, Worcester, Massachusetts

JOHN T. SCOTT—Professor of Political Science, University of California, Davis

SAMUEL A. STONER—Associate Professor of Philosophy, Assumption University, Worcester, Massachusetts

JOHN WARNER—Associate Professor of Political Science, Kansas State University, Manhattan, Kansas

ACKNOWLEDGMENTS

The essays in this volume were first presented at the 2023 A.V. Elliott Conference on Great Books and Ideas at Mercer University. This was an especially happy gathering because it marked the first time that the Elliott Conference had taken place live and in person since the beginning of the COVID-19 pandemic. The reunion of old friends and the making of new ones is an important part of the Elliott Conference experience, but it takes on special significance after two years of making due with a "virtual" experience. I therefore especially thank the contributors to this volume—Larry Cooper, Christine Dunn Henderson, Christopher Kelly, Emma Planinc, Denise Schaeffer, John Scott, Sam Stoner, and John Warner—for reenergizing the Elliott Conference and for working with me so diligently on this volume. I also thank Flora Champy, Daniel Cullen, Eve Grace, and Arthur Melzer for their excellent participation at the conference, as well as the panel of Mercer student scholars: Coy Eberhardt, Papa Guerrero, Michael Hurst, and Brandon Miley.

I also thank the A.V. Elliott family for the generous gift that continues to make the Elliott Conference and book series—this volume marks the twelfth book in the series—one of the nation's premier programs for the study of the history of political thought. Similarly, as co-director of the Thomas and Ramona McDonald Center for America's Founding Principles, I want to acknowledge the continuing generosity of Tom McDonald and the McDonald family, as they make possible all of our other important programing at Mercer. The work we do at the McDonald Center requires a great team, and I appreciate very much the work of my co-director Charlotte Thomas and the invaluable contributions of Kevin Honeycutt and Meg Donahue. And because it wouldn't be possible to accomplish any of these things without solid institutional backing, I appreciate very much the support provided over the years by Mercer President William Underwood and successive Deans of the College, Anita Gustafson and Thomas Scott.

In preparation for the 2023 Elliott Conference, a group of Mercer faculty and students convened over two semesters to read and discuss Rousseau's *Emile*, *Discourses*, and *Social Contract*. These conversations contributed in innumerable ways to the success of the project. I therefore thank Charlie Thomas, Kevin Honeycutt, Benjamin Hoyt, Tom Huber, Marc Jolley, Joseph Payne, David Swigart, Coy Eberhardt, Papa Guerrero, Anna Hale, Lillian Hall, Michael Hurst, Katherine Karbowski, Brandon Miley, Madeleine Pardue, Logan Scott, Jamie Stokes, Kate Van Meter, and Kendall Webb for their excellent reading and participation in this group.

Marc Jolley and his staff at Mercer University Press are also owed a debt of gratitude. As mentioned above, this is the twelfth volume in the series. Every one of these volumes presented unique challenges, but Marc and his staff always make sure things come together smoothly in the finished product. The ongoing success of this series is a testament to their consistently good work.

Finally, my deepest thanks are reserved for my wife Anissa and my sons Evan and Alex. Some debts are beyond the power of words.

INTRODUCTION

Will R. Jordan

Jean-Jacques Rousseau well understood that many readers would have trouble reconciling all of the apparent contradictions and inconsistencies found in his writings. In the middle of the *Social Contract*, for example, he pauses to assure his reader that "my ideas all fit together, but I cannot very well present them all at once."[1] But how do they all "fit together"? How *can* they? How are we to reconcile Rousseau's appeals to nature and to a natural man stripped "of all the supernatural gifts he could have received and of all the artificial faculties he could have acquired only by prolonged progress"[2] with his admiration for the rigorous and decidedly unnatural form of citizenship inculcated by regimes such as Sparta?[3] How are we to reconcile Rousseau's famous denigration of reason, and of the whole of the arts and sciences, with his appeals to thinkers such as Socrates and indeed to his own philosophic enterprise?[4] In short, how are we to reconcile the

---

[1] Jean-Jacques Rousseau, *On the Social Contract*, in *The Major Political Writings of Jean-Jacques Rousseau*, trans. John T. Scott (Chicago: University of Chicago Press, 2012), 187.

[2] Rousseau, *Discourse on the Origin and the Foundations of Inequality among Men*, in *The Major Political Writings*, 66.

[3] This tension between what is natural and what is necessary for true citizenship is made most explicitly in Book I of *Emile*. See, Jean-Jacques Rousseau, *Emile, or On Education*, trans. Allan Bloom (New York: Basic Books, 1979), 37–42.

[4] This tension is most clear in the *First Discourse*. See *Discourse on the Sciences and the Arts*, in *The Major Political Writings*, especially page 18 for his appeal to Socrates. Of course, the accompanying tension between philosophy and the city is made evident by any invocation of Socrates.

competing and seemingly irreconcilable visions of natural man, citizen, and philosopher that alternately surface and contend for preeminence in Rousseau's writings?

All of the essays in this volume take seriously Rousseau's claim that his "ideas all fit together," that his thought forms a coherent whole. They all wrestle, in one fashion or another, with the challenge of reconciling these disparate elements of his thought. One clear lesson that emerges from the essays is that while Rousseau's philosophic activity defies simple characterization, its highly idiosyncratic features are in many ways driven by the complexity of its subject. The apparent contradictions and tensions within Rousseau emerge through engagement with some of the most fundamental tensions of human life. Should we be understood and defined as individuals or as members of a community? How can we be free and live together? What in human beings is natural and what is the product of education, nurture, or historical processes? Are we defined more by our reason or by sentiment? How do we come to know something and how might our attempts to know potentially undermine truth itself? In working through all of these problems, the Rousseau that emerges is truly a thinker of the first rank, a subtle and penetrating student of what it means to be a human being, a citizen, and a philosopher.

In the first chapter, "Rousseau's Freedom: Phenomenological, Not Metaphysical," John T. Scott examines an important characteristic of Rousseau's approach to philosophy and does so by examining Rousseau's treatment of the concept of freedom. Against scholars who find in Rousseau either a thoroughgoing materialism or a metaphysical dualism (with its clear division of body from soul or spirit), Scott argues that Rousseau avoids making a commitment to such an abstract or theoretical proposition. Instead, Scott finds that Rousseau grounds his concept of freedom in a more practical, phenomenological way—in the *experience* of a "recognition, consciousness, or feeling" of choice. Scott traces the development of this experience of freedom through the *Discourse on Inequality*, the "Profession of Faith of the Savoyard Vicar" in *Emile*, and finally to the forms of natural, civil, and moral freedom discussed in the *Social Contract*. Scott's approach resolves several of the apparent inconsistencies that others have found in Rousseau's understanding of what it means to be free.

Laurence D. Cooper continues the exploration of the unique features of Rousseau's approach to philosophy in his chapter, "The Philosopher as Natural Man." Starting from the seemingly obvious incompatibility between Rousseau's conception of nature and the life of philosophy (the *Discourses* go so far as to suggest that the development of reason and philosophy tear people away from both natural goodness and civic virtue), Cooper argues that a more careful reading of Rousseau's corpus, and especially *The Reveries of the Solitary Walker*, reveals a way in which philosophy can be made compatible with, and even represent the fulfillment of, man's nature. Some features of Rousseau's healthy philosophy include that it is animated by natural self-love (rather than a debased and rivalrous amour-propre), that it develops the best of our natural dispositions and potentialities, and that it intensifies and deepens our identification with the whole of nature. The Rousseau that emerges here holds a view of nature that is much closer to the teleological view of classical philosophy than is usually supposed.

In the following chapter, Emma Planinc offers a reading of the *Second Discourse* that challenges the familiar dichotomy (discussed in Cooper's piece) between natural and healthy love of self (*amour-de-soi-même*) and the comparative vanity of amour-propre. As indicated by her title, "Pride Precedes the Ruin of the

Soul: On Rousseau's use of *orgueil* in the *Second Discourse*," Planinc contends that it is actually a third form of self-love—pride (or *orgueil*)—that best explains the structure of the *Second Discourse*. This form of pride is the unnatural tendency for human beings to set their own *species* above the rest of nature and carries with it the explicitly biblical connotation of sinfulness. In Planinc's account, part 1 and part 2 of the *Second Discourse* tell the same story, but the first version (without *orgueil*) describes man as part of the order of nature, while part 2 (with *orgueil*) begins with man sinfully considering mankind to be superior to the rest of creation. This reading of the *Second Discourse* sees Rousseau offering his own alternative version of the biblical story of original sin, as well as his own solution to it.

We return to the question of the naturalness of philosophy in Samuel Stoner's "The Problem of Knowledge in Rousseau's *Second Discourse*." Stoner shows Rousseau's debt to Rene Descartes in pursuing a philosophic method that strips human beings of all unreliable customs and opinions in order to arrive at a more certain foundation of knowledge. However, Rousseau's final stopping point at the "still soul of natural man" goes so far as to undermine even Descartes's *cogito* by calling into question the naturalness of thinking and philosophic knowledge itself. In Stoner's view, Rousseau's critique of reason and introduction of the idea that reason itself is subject to historical processes represent important departures from Descartes (and perhaps create some tension with Cooper's argument about Rousseau and the naturalness of philosophy). However, Stoner ends his piece with the intriguing suggestion that Rousseau's radical new deployment of Descartes's method may in fact undermine itself, by revealing its inability to account for the origin of knowledge. If this is right, Rousseau may be subtly calling into question the possibility of ever attaining the sort of certainty promised by his method.

Another difficulty posed by reason is discussed in John Warner's "Sincerity and Self-Deception in *The Profession of Faith of the Savoyard Vicar.*" Warner analyzes this famous and much-debated subsection of Rousseau's *Emile* by contesting the claims that the vicar is a model of sincerity and that he serves as a mouthpiece for Rousseau. Warner's careful reading reveals that the vicar is in fact guilty of self-deception (a quality greatly at odds with Rousseau's professed preference for sincerity) and willingly sacrifices truth for the sake of his own self-esteem as well as the relief of his own metaphysical anxiety. However, despite the unattractiveness of the vicar's hypocritical self-deception, Warner suggests that it is still possible to read him as a sort of exemplar for Rousseau, but now as one that reveals what is required to make religious belief useful even if it fails to be true in any ultimate sense. This final claim may help inform Rousseau's arguments about the role of religion in his political philosophy.

We stay with Rousseau's great treatise on education for Denise Schaeffer's "Travel as Philosophic Education in *Emile.*" Schaeffer focuses on book five of *Emile* and examines the several places in this book that discuss travel, including those outside of the subsection explicitly dedicated to this subject. What emerges is a careful study of the proper object and form of travel, as well as an identification of the major obstacles to travel done well. Of particular interest is the tension between learning about the real peculiarities of places and learning to see "men in general." Schaeffer advances the compelling argument that Rousseau's account of travel serves as the capstone to Emile's philosophic education. In becoming a philosopher, it is necessary to reach for a standard beyond the parochial, but Schaeffer shows us that Rousseau is equally concerned with the danger of philosophers becoming idealistically detached from the world as it actually exists around us. Rousseau's "carefully calculated middle distance" helps resolve the potential conflict between philosopher and citizen by teaching his reader the necessity of combining both through the practice of political philosophy properly understood.

Christopher Kelly offers a delightful reading of one of Rousseau's most obscure and confounding works in his chapter, "Misunderstanding Rousseau: The Enigmas of *Rousseau: Judge of Jean-Jacques*." We return here to the subjects of how to understand Rousseau's peculiar philosophic project and how this project put him at odds with the society in which he lived. But now, the text being analyzed is a dialogue between a Frenchman and a man named "Rousseau" (who isn't quite Jean-Jacques Rousseau) about a controversial author named "Jean-Jacques" (who also isn't quite Jean-Jacques Rousseau). Kelly guides us through a series of enigmas that provide the key to unlocking this text. All of these enigmas result in a defense of a particular way of life—a philosophy of natural goodness—that serves as an "alternative to both Christianity and to modern anti-Christian doctrines." Although the tension between philosophy and the city is as old as Socrates, of particular interest here is Rousseau's account of how modern public opinion makes this problem especially acute.

Rousseau's influence on the history of political thought was immense, and in the last chapter—"Tocqueville's Reveries: On the condition of women and the influence of Rousseau"—Christine Dunn Henderson works through one example of this broad influence. Henderson is struck by Alexis de Tocqueville's description of the differing condition of American girls and American women. The relative freedom of the former is lost when the latter retreat into the confines of the "domestic cloister." Though Tocqueville is largely complimentary of this development, Henderson points out how this conclusion does not quite fit with other important elements of Tocqueville's analysis—including his worries about the division of labor, the dangers of an individualistic retreat from the public sphere, and the tyrannical social pressure exerted by democratic majorities. Henderson accounts for Tocqueville's inconsistency here by finding an overreliance on the framework established for the education of women in Rousseau's *Emile*. However, she also notes that had Tocqueville been a more careful reader of Rousseau, he might have found grounds for a less restrictive view of women's possible roles in society.

Certainly, the eight chapters contained in this book range across many of Rousseau's works and touch on a wide variety of important themes in his political thought. Perhaps the most common thread, however, is an appreciation for the subtlety and singularity of Rousseau's philosophic approach. Rousseau's writings include deep reflection on what it means to be a philosopher and a keen awareness of how complicated the relationship is between the philosopher, the citizen, and the man of natural goodness. Yet, Rousseau, somehow, strives to unify and embody all three of these ideals at the same time.

1.

ROUSSEAU'S FREEDOM: PHENOMENOLOGICAL, NOT METAPHYSICAL

John T. Scott

Freedom or liberty (*liberté*) is self-evidently a critical concept in Rousseau's thought. In the *Discourse on Inequality* he writes of the loss of freedom upon entering civil society: "as an untamed steed bristles his mane, stamps the ground with its hoof, and struggles impetuously at the very approach of a bit...so barbarous man does not bend his head for the yoke civilized man wears without a murmur, and he prefers the most turbulent freedom to a tranquil subjection" (*SD*, 108).[1] In the *Social Contract* he famously declares: "man is born free, and everywhere he is in chains" (*SC*, I.1.163).[2] Later in the work he explains what these chains mean: "to renounce one's freedom is to renounce one's quality as a man, the rights of humanity, even its duties" (*SC*, I.4.168). And, finally, he infamously proclaims that whoever refuses to obey his general will as a citizen will be "forced to be free" (*SC*, I.7.175). As this

---

[1] *SD*, cited by page, will refer to the *Discourse on Inequality*, or *Second Discourse*, in: Jean-Jacques Rousseau, *The Major Political Writings of Jean-Jacques Rousseau*, trans. and ed. John T. Scott (Chicago: University of Chicago Press, 2012). I have altered all translations where necessary without so noting based on Rousseau, *Œuvres complètes*, ed. Bernard Gagnebin and Marcel Raymond, 5 vols. (Paris: Gallimard, Bibliothèque de la Pléiade, 1959–95).

[2] Hereafter, *SC*, cited by book, chapter, and page, refers to the *Social Contract* in Rousseau, *Major Political Writings*.

brief survey of some of Rousseau's best-known statements shows, however, while freedom may be a critical concept in his thought, it is not at all self-evident how Rousseau understands freedom.

In this chapter I develop an interpretation of Rousseau's conception of freedom. While my interpretation throws light on Rousseau's various discussions of freedom in his works, and especially the distinction he draws in his political treatise among natural freedom, civil freedom, and moral freedom, my principal aim here is to focus on his understanding of our *experience* of freedom. My argument is that for Rousseau freedom is something we experience phenomenologically and, further, that he advances his conception of freedom in its various forms in a metaphysically neutral manner. My title is meant to invoke John Rawls's well-known essay "Justice as Fairness: Political not Metaphysical."[3] Rawls argues there that the theory of "justice as fairness" formulated in his *Theory of Justice* does not depend upon any controversial philosophical or metaphysical assumptions and is instead meant to be a public conception of justice which can be widely accepted in a constitutional democracy. Rousseau likewise generally avoids metaphysical debates concerning freedom, and arguably for similar reasons. His strategy is exemplified in the *Discourse on Inequality* when he steps away from an initial argument that freedom distinguishes humans from the other animals because of the "difficulties" involved with such a claim, that is metaphysical difficulties, and instead claims that humans are distinguished by "perfectibility" (*SD*, 71–72). Examining this passage concerning freedom and others, I show that Rousseau instead understands freedom phenomenologically: as an experience of becoming self-conscious about our capacity to choose.

---

[3] John Rawls, "Justice as Fairness: Political not Metaphysical," *Philosophy and Public Affairs* 14 (1985): 223–51.

The question of the metaphysical basis for Rousseau's conception of freedom, and indeed his theory of human nature in general, has been the subject of continuing scholarly debate. The spectrum of answers is wide and diverse, ranging from those who argue that Rousseau is a materialist all the way to those who contend he embraces metaphysical dualism.[4] Part of the reason for this disagreement is the view of some that Rousseau's position shifts across his writing, moving from a naturalist or even materialist stance in the *Discourse on Inequality* to the embrace of metaphysical dualism in his later educational treatise, *Emile*.[5] More specifically, those who argue that Rousseau is a dualist in the later work rely upon the arguments contained in the "Profession of Faith of the Savoyard Vicar," a separate section of the treatise containing a lengthy theological meditation by a Catholic priest. The separate status of the "Profession" raises a number of interpretive hurdles I will discuss later, but for now it suffices to say two things. First, that the dualism of the "Profession" is an odd fit with the rest of *Emile*, which does not propound any clear metaphysics, much less a dualist one. Second, the fact that Rousseau does not present the "Profession" in his own voice calls into

---

[4] For materialist interpretations, see Marc Plattner, *Rousseau's State of Nature: An Interpretation of the Discourse on Inequality* (Dekalb: Northern Illinois University Press, 1979); Jared Holley, "Rousseau on Refined Epicureanism and the Problem of Modern Liberty," *European Journal of Political Theory* 17 (2019): 411–31. For dualist interpretations, see Timothy O'Hagan, "Taking Rousseau Seriously," *History of Political Thought* 25 (2004): 73–85; Robin Douglass, "Free Will and the Problem of Evil: Reconciling Rousseau's Divided Thought," *History of Political Thought* 31 (2010): 639–55; Lee MacLean, *The Free Animal: Rousseau on Free Will and Human Nature* (Toronto: University of Toronto Press, 2013).

[5] See Timothy O'Hagan, *Rousseau* (London: Routledge, 1999); Christopher Brooke, "Jean-Jacques Rousseau," chap. 8 in *Philosophic Pride: Stoicism and Political Thought from Lipsius to Rousseau* (Princeton: Princeton University Press, 2012).

question where he himself stands on these issues. Due to these many interpretive complexities, among other reasons, some scholars sit out this debate and argue that Rousseau intentionally presents his conceptions of freedom and of human nature in a metaphysically neutral manner.[6] I largely follow in the footsteps of these scholars but add the critical argument that the essence of Rousseau's conception of freedom is phenomenological rather than metaphysical.[7]

I begin with an analysis of one of Rousseau's most important discussions of freedom, namely the passage from the *Discourse on Inequality* mentioned above where he first posits that free will distinguishes humans from the animals only to withdraw or at least amend that claim. I draw particular attention to two aspects of that passage: the relationship of freedom to perfectibility and the importance of his remarks about the "consciousness" of our freedom ultimately distinguishing us from the animals, both of which aspects relate to what I am terming his phenomenological account of freedom. I then turn briefly to the discussion of freedom in the "Profession of Faith" in *Emile*, partly to bracket the metaphysical account of freedom there due to the interpretive hurdles already mentioned, but also to show how the account there can be reread as a phenomenological rather than metaphysical one. I then turn to Rousseau's discussion in the *Social Contract*

---

[6] See Leo Strauss, *Natural Right and History* (Chicago: University of Chicago Press, 1953), 255–56; Roger D. Masters, *The Political Philosophy of Rousseau* (Princeton: Princeton University Press, 1968), 69–71. Masters argues that the "Profession" contains a "detachable metaphysics" to which Rousseau himself may subscribe, but not one upon which he builds his philosophy. See *Political Philosophy of Rousseau*, 58–73.

[7] In a previous work I suggest a phenomenological interpretation of human nature in Rousseau, but do not develop the idea with regard to freedom. See John T. Scott, *Rousseau's God: Theology, Religion, and the Natural Goodness of Man* (Chicago: University of Chicago Press, 2023), 112–24.

of freedom, namely the distinction he draws among natural freedom, civil freedom, and moral freedom. I suggest that his brief remarks concerning "moral freedom" have been misinterpreted and instead argue that a phenomenological interpretation of moral freedom is more accurate and in keeping with what Rousseau argues elsewhere in his writings.

Freedom in the *Discourse on Inequality*

The first glimpse of freedom in the *Discourse on Inequality* comes immediately, in both the frontispiece and the Dedication to the work. We see there a Hottentot who has tossed a bundle of clothing to the ground with a number of Dutchmen behind him witnessing the act. In the note to which Rousseau refers the reader in a caption to the frontispiece we learn that the Hottentot was raised and educated in the European manner but has decided to return to his fellow Hottentots. The caption on the frontispiece reads: "he goes back to his equals" (*SD*, 38). As the frontispiece for a work devoted to the question of inequality, this caption is apt. But the story is also one of freedom: throwing off the shackles of civil society and returning to the state of nature, insofar as that is possible (*SD*, 116). In the Dedication to the City of Geneva, in turn, we see civil freedom in the form of the self-legislation by the citizens and the independence of the city from external powers, a condition for self-legislation. Rousseau does not affirm that his native city fully enjoys this civil freedom, and in fact it is Rome, not Geneva, which he declares is the "model for all free peoples" (*SD*, 43). Modern peoples, even Geneva, enjoy at best a faded and fragile form of civil freedom.

The way in which Rousseau raises the issue of freedom in the Preface to the *Discourse* begins to raise more philosophically weighted issues which will take us to Rousseau's most extensive discussion of freedom in the work, which will be my focus. There he takes up the question posed by the Academy of Dijon concerning the origin of inequality and especially of whether inequality is authorized by the natural law, a discussion which effectively puts aside the question of natural law. Remarking on the interminable and inconclusive debates over natural law, Rousseau states that for natural law to be a "law" in any meaningful way, it must be "a rule prescribed to a moral being—that is, a being that is intelligent, free, and considered in its relations with other beings." If so, then animals cannot be subject to natural law because they lack reason. But the same would be true of humans prior to the full development of reason. The question of metaphysics enters at this point. "But while each defines this law after his own fashion, all of them base it on such metaphysical principles that even among us there are very few people capable of comprehending these principles, far from being able to discover them by themselves." Such an approach to natural law would require being "a very great reasoner and profound metaphysician" to understand it and to obey it. Rousseau thus dismisses natural law and the metaphysical questions it raises and instead appeals to experience. We are subject not to a natural law we cannot comprehend, but instead to natural right, a right based on the primary "principles" of self-love and pity. We are subject to natural right as "sensitive beings," and therefore so are the animals, after a fashion (*SD*, 53–55). Natural right requires only that we feel, and if reason must reestablish the rules of natural right after our natural feelings are stifled, as Rousseau states (*SD*, 55), it does not require doing so on the basis of any particular metaphysics.

Rousseau's substantive discussion of freedom comes when he turns from the "physical man" he has been describing to this point in the work, namely natural man in the pure state of nature, to look at this being "from the metaphysical and moral side" (*SD*, 71). Before examining this important discussion, some clarifications concerning terminology are necessary. What does Rousseau mean by "metaphysical" and "moral"?[8]

Given my subject in this chapter, the term "metaphysical" (*métaphysique*) is particularly important to clarify. In the usage of Rousseau's time, in the broadest sense, "metaphysical" is nearly synonymous with what we would mean by "psychological." Rousseau never uses the words "psychology" or "psychological" in any of his writings, as far as I am aware, even though they were available to him, although only recently. The connection between "metaphysics" and what we would call psychology is evident in d'Alembert's "Preliminary Discourse" to the *Encyclopédie* (1751): "In a word, [Locke] reduced metaphysics to what it in fact ought to be: the experimental physics of the soul."[9] This meaning of "metaphysical" as the study of how sensations give rise to ideas explains why Rousseau's exposition of man from the "metaphysical and moral side" is followed by a discussion of language and reason. D'Alembert's remark about how metaphysics ought to be pursued suggests that there are incorrect approaches, or at least other approaches, to the subject. These are "metaphysical" debates concerning free will, the nature of the soul, substances, etc., or "metaphysics" in what might be termed a narrow sense. As for Rousseau, his discussion of man "from the metaphysical and moral side" will encompass "metaphysics" in both the broad and the narrow meanings.

As for the term "moral" (*morale*), it is not restricted to what we would call "morality," but is nearly synonymous with "social." Something of this sense of the term is evident if we consider that *morale* and *moralité* are etymologically related to *moeurs*, another

---

[8] For a more extensive discussion of Rousseau's terminology, see Scott, *Rousseau's God*, 109–11.

[9] Quoted in Victor Goldschmidt, *Anthropologie et politique: Les principes du système de Rousseau* (Paris: Vrin, 1974), 267n51.

word difficult to translate, but roughly the mores or manners we observe in our social and moral relations. As with the term "metaphysical," Rousseau's examination of man from the "moral side" includes broad matters concerning moral or social relations of all sorts and questions of morality in the narrower sense. Let us now turn to his examination of man "from the metaphysical and moral side."

Rousseau begins his investigation by attempting to discern what distinguishes humans from the other animals. "I see in every animal only an ingenious machine to which nature has given senses to revitalize itself and protect itself, up to a certain point, from everything that tends to destroy or disturb it," he commences. "I perceive precisely the same things in the human machine, with this difference: that nature alone does everything in the operations of the beast whereas man contributes to his own operations in his capacity as a free agent." To illustrate this claim, he offers a comparison between the behavior of two animals, a pigeon and a cat, and humans. Whereas the two animals are confined by their instinctually fixed preference for a certain type of food, humans will eat anything and, in fact, dissolutely give themselves over to excessive eating, "because the mind depraves the senses, and because the will still speaks when nature is silent" (*SD*, 71).

Let me begin by observing something not often remarked upon about this passage: Rousseau bases his claim on empirical observation. Hence his first words: "I see," and then later, "I perceive." There is a slight difference here, however, for "to see" (*voir*) is unambiguously an empirical matter, whereas "to perceive" (*appercevoir*) can involve either simple sight or something more like a matter of intellection, to glimpse with the mind's eye. Hence Rousseau's earlier claim that "meditating on the first and simplest operations of the human soul, I believe I perceive in it two principles preceding reason" (*SD*, 54). Be that as it may, there is as yet no appeal to metaphysics to explain the difference between man and animal. The claim about man being a "free agent" is thus far based on observation and experience concerning dietary choices by animals and humans.

But what does Rousseau's example actually prove? Does man, or at least natural man, exercise free will in any meaningful way? Or does he have very limited instinct, here with regard to diet, even to the point of lacking instinct? The second alternative is suggested by an earlier example from the *Discourse* concerning natural man's diet. "Men, dispersed among [the animals], observe and imitate their industry, and so raise themselves up to the level of the instinct of beasts, with the advantage that each species has only its own instinct, and man—perhaps having none that belongs to him—appropriates them all to himself, feeds himself equally well on most of the various foods which the other animals divide among themselves, and consequently finds his subsistence more easily than any of them can" (*SD*, 66). Rousseau hedges here and elsewhere concerning human instinct: man "perhaps" has no instinct. He will return to the question of instinct after positing perfectibility as the distinctive human trait: "savage man, left by nature to instinct alone, or rather compensated for that instinct he perhaps lacks by faculties capable of substituting for it at first and then of raising him far above nature, will therefore begin with purely animal functions. To perceive and to feel will be his first state, which he will have in common with all the animals. To will and not to will, to desire and to fear, will be the first and almost the only operations of his soul until new circumstances cause new developments in it" (*SD*, 73). Are "willing" and "not willing" distinctively human, or are they among the "purely animal functions" man shares with the animals? The latter reading would make sense if "to desire" and "to fear" are effectively renaming "to will" and "not to will." Does the instinct savage man "perhaps" lacks serve as the condition for the capacity for choice, for example with regard to food, however we might understand the basis and character of such choice by savage man?

After adducing the different dietary behaviors of humans and animals as evidence that man is a free agent, Rousseau proceeds in a more metaphysical vein, meaning "metaphysical" in both the broad and narrow senses I have identified. "Every animal has ideas since it has senses, it even combines its ideas up to a certain point, and man differs in this regard from beast only by degree.... It is therefore not so much understanding that constitutes the specific difference of man among the animals" (*SD*, 71–72). Here we have a "metaphysical" explanation in the broad sense of mental or psychological processes. Note the qualification: it is not "so much" understanding that distinguishes humans. In other words, it does so distinguish them, at least as a matter of degree if not kind, since animals combine ideas "up to a certain point." Perhaps the (ultimate) human capacity to combine ideas in a more complex manner is related to the more extensive capacity for choice. If it is not so much understanding that distinguishes human beings, Rousseau now makes a bolder pronouncement: "it is his capacity as a free agent." He explains:

> Nature commands every animal, and the beast obeys. Man feels the same impetus, but he recognizes that he is free to acquiesce or resist, and it is above all in the consciousness of this freedom that the spirituality of his soul is shown: for physics in a way explains the mechanics of the senses and the formation of ideas, but in the power of willing, or rather of choosing, and in the feeling of this power are found only spiritual acts, about which nothing is explained by the laws of mechanics. (*SD*, 72)

This passage contains Rousseau's most extensive remarks about human freedom.

This passage has been adduced by interpreters as evidence that Rousseau embraces a dualist metaphysics, and understandably so. He seems to distinguish between psychological processes which can be explained at least "in a way" (*en quelque manière*) in terms of physics or mechanics, namely the senses and formation of ideas which man shares with the animals, on the one hand, from "the power of willing, or rather of choosing," which is a "spiritual act" that cannot be explained in terms of physics or mechanics, on the other. The passage therefore invites us to assume a distinction between soul and body familiar to various forms of dualism. Yet several details of the passage might give us pause in taking him up on this invitation. First, by substituting "choosing" for "willing," Rousseau seems to back away from the swampy terrain surrounding the question of free will, a central feature of dualist metaphysics, for the firmer ground of "choosing," which seems to be a psychological or mental operation, and perhaps one which can be explained in terms of physics or mechanics in some fashion. Second, he does not explain what he means by a "spiritual act" or the "spirituality" of the soul. Indeed, nowhere else in his writings does he use such terminology, with the exception of stating in the chapter "On Civil Religion" in the *Social Contract* that Jesus established a "spiritual kingdom on earth" (*SC*, IV.8.265). This is not a complementary employment of "spiritual." Third, when he contrasts beast and man in this paragraph, with the beast obeying nature and man recognizing he is free to choose, he seems to restate what he wrote in the previous paragraph concerning the fixed dietary regime of cats and pigeons as opposed to the man who chooses "in his capacity as a free agent," but with a revealing addition. Namely, he speaks of the human who "recognizes" (*se reconnoît*) that he is free to acquiesce or resist and who has "consciousness" (*conscience*) of this freedom or who has the "feeling" (*sentiment*) of this power.

If the *recognition* or *consciousness* or *feeling* of our power of willing or choosing is what is distinctively human, then a phenomenological reading of this passage concerning freedom becomes inviting. Such a reading would also not require any particular metaphysical commitment on Rousseau's part to explain such consciousness. At any rate, Rousseau himself withdraws from the ontological battlefield at this point. "But, even if the difficulties surrounding all these questions should leave some room for dispute concerning this difference between man and animal," he begins the next paragraph, "there is another very specific quality that distinguishes them and about which there can be no argument: that is, the faculty of perfecting himself—a faculty which, with the aid of circumstances, successively develops all the others" (*SD*, 72). The "difficulties" are, of course, the thorny questions of metaphysics. Apparently, there can be no argument about this distinctively human capacity because it is an empirically observed phenomenon, and Rousseau therefore glosses his claim by pointing out that an individual animal and a given species do not develop beyond a fixed point of maturity whereas humans do develop both as individuals and as a species. In the language I have been using, "perfectibility," as Rousseau now neologistically names it, is a phenomenological claim, not a metaphysical one.[10]

If savage man begins with "purely animal functions," perfectibility makes it possible for him to develop, or rather perfectibility names this unique capacity for development. Rousseau describes a dynamic relationship among needs, passions, and reason (and related faculties) which, once set into motion "with the aid of circumstances," makes such development possible (*SD*, 73). Since he

[10] Goldschmidt states that perfectibility is "incontestable and metaphysically neutral" (*Anthropologie et politique*, 292).

"perhaps" lacks instincts and begins with "purely animal functions," as Rousseau writes immediately before describing this dynamic relationship, man has needs and means for satisfying those needs which are far more plastic than those of the other animals, making this dynamic possible. If he begins with "purely animal functions," those functions develop in a way that distinguishes him from the animals. What about consciousness of the power to will or choose? Rousseau describes savage man: "his soul, which nothing agitates, gives itself over to the sole feeling [*sentiment*] of its present existence, without any idea of the future" (*SD*, 74). Savage man lacks the feeling or sentiment of his power to will or choose; his soul is far from "spiritual." However, perfectibility enables him to develop in such a way that he can experience this recognition, consciousness, or feeling.

What, then, is the relationship between freedom and perfectibility? Interpreters generally fall into two camps which align with their positions on his metaphysical stance or lack thereof. On the one hand, some interpreters argue that Rousseau effectively abandons his claim about humans being distinguished from the animals by being "free agents" and especially the dualist metaphysics that the claim seems to entail and, given the "difficulties" with such a claim, turns instead to perfectibility as what is distinctively human. These interpreters often further argue that perfectibility does not rest on any particular metaphysical basis.[11] On the other hand, other scholars claim that Rousseau does not abandon his claim about freedom, or a dualist metaphysics, and instead argue that his argument concerning perfectibility is a

[11] See Strauss, *Natural Right and History*, 265–66; Goldschmidt, *Anthropologie et politique*, 288–97; Masters, *Political Philosophy of Rousseau*, 69–71; Plattner, *Rousseau's State of Nature*, 43–46.

continuation of, not a break from, the argument about freedom and its "spiritual" character.[12]

Let me suggest something of a middle road between these two camps. My analysis suggests that Rousseau's conception of freedom as he advances it in the *Discourse on Inequality* is better understood as phenomenological and not metaphysical. I have further argued that his apparent dualism is severely attenuated upon closer examination and that he puts aside whatever metaphysical claims he tentatively advances and instead identifies perfectibility as the distinctively human attribute. To this extent I follow the first set of scholars. However, I join the second set in suggesting that freedom and perfectibility should be interpreted in light of one another, but I do so by reversing the direction. Namely, instead of interpreting perfectibility in light of freedom, and especially any metaphysical claims about freedom, I suggest that freedom should be interpreted in light of perfectibility. For Rousseau, freedom—along with reason, speech, and the other attributes that previous philosophers have long argued distinguish humans from the other animals—is grounded in perfectibility as potential developments of human nature.[13] As for freedom in particular, I suggest that the capacity for psychological development named by perfectibility eventually enables humans to experience the recognition, consciousness, and feeling of their freedom, as a matter of experience, as phenomenological and not metaphysical.

---

[12] See Douglass, "Free Will and the Problem of Evil"; MacLean, "Interpreting Free Will and Perfectibility in the *Discourse on Inequality*," chap. 1 in *The Free Animal*; O'Hagan, "Taking Rousseau Seriously."

[13] See John T. Scott, "The Paradoxical Perfection of *Perfectibilité*: From Rousseau to Condorcet," *History of European Ideas* 50, no. 2 (2024): 211–27.

Freedom in *Emile*

Recognizing some of the ambiguities or hesitations in Rousseau's discussion in the *Discourse on Inequality* of freedom and its possible metaphysical basis, scholars seeking a metaphysical interpretation of freedom in Rousseau's thought often turn to his educational treatise, *Emile*, and especially to the meditations on the soul, freedom, and conscience in the "Profession of Faith of the Savoyard Vicar." As mentioned at the outset, the "Profession" is an explicitly separate section of *Emile* which is purportedly a "paper" written by a separate "author" which reports the events of three decades earlier, most importantly a recollection of the profession of faith delivered to him by a Savoyard Vicar. Rousseau serves as the editor of the writing, for example adding footnotes to the Vicar's speech. He attests to the truth of the facts related in the paper he is about to transcribe, but he does not attest to the truth of the substance of the Vicar's speech, and instead states that he provides it for any "useful reflections" the reader might take from it (*E*, 260).[14] There is considerable disagreement among scholars about how to assess the relationship of the "Profession" to what Rousseau writes in his own name, including on questions of metaphysics. On one extreme of the spectrum scholars simply take the "Profession" as containing Rousseau's own views, and indeed his most fully articulated conception of metaphysical and other philosophical issues. On the other extreme, interpreters do not regard the Vicar as speaking for Rousseau, and for a number of reasons, including the textual separateness of the "Profession," and the contradictions or tensions between the Vicar's arguments and what Rousseau writes in his own name, and other reasons.

[14]*E* refers to Rousseau, *Emile, or On Education*, trans. Allan Bloom (New York: Basic Books, 1979), cited by page.

Since I have written extensively on the "Profession" and the interpretive debates over the work, I will not enter into the details here about issues either of substance or scholarship. My view is that the "Profession" serves a different purpose from the main text of *Emile* and is directed at a different audience, with the rhetorical demands of the audience and the purpose of the writing explaining the substance of the arguments advanced by the Vicar, which differ in decisive respects from what Rousseau himself argues.[15] To put my argument in the terms of the present analysis, whereas the Vicar's conception of freedom, the soul, and conscience entails a form of dualist metaphysics, Rousseau's approach to these subjects is phenomenological and not metaphysical. My analysis of Rousseau's conception of freedom and related issues as it comes to light in *Emile* will therefore be brief. First, I will examine an illuminating passage in the main text of *Emile* to see what Rousseau writes in his own name in the work. Second, I will examine a parallel passage in the "Profession of Faith," first showing how the Vicar's argument differs in terms of metaphysical commitments from what Rousseau himself writes and then suggesting how or to what degree the Vicar's argument could be reinterpreted in a phenomenological mode.

The passage I want to examine in the main text of *Emile* concerns consciousness and metaphysics. Well, not precisely "consciousness" but rather "conscience," both words being the same in French: *conscience*. The passage is in book four of *Emile*, which is devoted to the dawn of adolescence, the development of the passions, and the recognition of other human beings through pity (and sexual love).

[15] See Scott, *Rousseau's God*, chaps. 5–6, for a more extensive interpretation of *Emile* and the "Profession," and the relationship between them.

> If this were the place for it, I would try to show how the first voices of conscience [*conscience*] arise out of the first movement of the heart, and how the first notions of good and bad are born of the sentiments of love and hate. I would show that *justice* and *goodness* are not merely abstract words—pure moral beings formed by the understanding—but are true affections of the soul enlightened by reason, and hence only an ordered development of our primitive affections; that by reason alone, independent of conscience, no natural law can be established; and the entire right of nature is only a chimera if it is not founded on a natural need of the human heart.* But I am reminded that my business here is not producing treatises on metaphysics and morals. (*E*, 235)

Although Rousseau disclaims the notion that he is producing a treatise on "metaphysics and morals," he is in fact doing so after a fashion. Keeping in mind the broad and narrow senses of both "metaphysics" and "morals" here is important. Good to his word, Rousseau is not developing a metaphysical doctrine in the narrow sense of the term, at least in any explicit way, and he is definitely not advancing a dualist metaphysics. However, he is putting forward a metaphysical position in the broad sense of the term. Namely, he is arguing that moral phenomena, here justice and goodness, arise out of what we might call psychological phenomena, here the "first movements of the heart" and the sentiments of love and hate, which would appear to stem from the primary principles of self-love and pity as they develop into "true affections of the soul enlightened by reason." In this way, then, "metaphysics" in the broad sense of psychological serves as the basis for the "moral" aspects of human nature in the narrow sense of the term. As for the "conscience" (*conscience*), this passage suggests that it, too, is based on the primary principles of self-love and pity as they develop along with reason and the other faculties, and I would suggest along with "consciousness" (*conscience*). This reading is borne out in the note Rousseau adds to the passage (marked by the asterisk toward the end) in which he writes: "even the precept of doing unto others as we would have them do unto us has no true foundation other than conscience and sentiment.... Love of men derived from love of self is the principle of human justice" (*E*, 235n). At any rate, there is no hint of metaphysical dualism in Rousseau's non-treatise on metaphysics and morals or in his treatment of conscience there.

Let me now turn to the treatment of these same topics in the "Profession." First, a general remark. Although the Savoyard Vicar's reasoning does eventuate in a dualist metaphysics of two substances, material body and immaterial soul, he does not begin with or advance this dualism as an a priori principle but instead proceeds in what might be characterized as an a posteriori manner. He arrives at dualism out of two related concerns. First, he needs to explain the moral disorder he sees among humans, and he adduces "two principles" to explain the origin of moral evil in human freedom (*E*, 278–79). Second, dualism explains his experience, in this case his experience of dividedness, a tension between his body and his soul. In this sense, then, his entire approach might be characterized as less metaphysical (in the narrow sense of the term) than phenomenological. In this way, the distance between Rousseau and the Vicar potentially narrows.

At this point in his argument, the Vicar entertains the opposed alternatives of materialism and dualism. He admits that these metaphysical issues are beyond his comprehension, but he opts for dualism because he feels it better explains his experience. Specifically, he experiences his "power to will" and the "sentiment of my freedom" (*E*, 280). These experiences could be reframed in terms of the recognition, consciousness, and feeling or sentiment of the power to choose or will that we saw in the *Discourse on Inequality*, without any metaphysical commitment. Likewise, the Vicar's account of "goodness" and "justice" (*E*, 282) could be reframed in the way Rousseau himself does in his own name in the passage from *Emile* examined above. The Vicar claims that the problem of theodicy which led him to adopt a dualist metaphysics in the first place, namely the existence of evil despite a beneficent divinity, is best explained by dualism. "But this question is no longer a difficulty for me as soon as I have acknowledged two substances" (*E*, 283). Finally, when he turns to the rules of conduct he draws from his metaphysical meditations, the Vicar appeals to the conscience. "Conscience is the voice of the soul; the passions are the voice of the body. Is it surprising that these two languages often are contradictory" (*E*, 286). Once again, the Vicar's account of conscience could be reframed in the way Rousseau himself does, again without any dualist metaphysics. If the Vicar turns to a dualist metaphysics to explain the contradictions he experiences within himself, we should remind ourselves that the very aim of the education Emile receives is to prevent such dividedness and instead to preserve his natural unity.

Freedom in the *Social Contract*

How to find a form of political association whose members obey only themselves and remain as free as they were before? What does it mean to "force" someone to be "free" if they decide to follow their particular will as a man rather than their general will as a citizen? The *Social Contract* poses a number of difficult interpretive questions related to Rousseau's conception of freedom. My focus here will be narrow, namely an examination of the distinction he draws in the work among three types of freedom: natural, civil, and moral. For it is moral freedom in particular which has been interpreted in light of the philosophical and metaphysical issues in Rousseau's thought to which I have attended. Namely, a number of interpreters have claimed that Rousseau's conception of moral freedom relies upon a dualist metaphysics they see in the *Discourse on Inequality* and especially the "Profession" in *Emile.*[16] Similarly, without such a strong argument concerning the metaphysical commitments necessary for moral freedom, other interpreters have read Rousseau's conception of freedom through a Kantian lens of idealism.[17] In my view, both the dualist and Kantian readings of moral freedom are incorrect, and I instead suggest a phenomenological approach.

Rousseau's enumeration of three kinds of freedom—natural, civil, and moral—occurs in book 1, chapter 8 of the *Social Contract*: "On the Civil State." This chapter is the culmination of a trio of chapters beginning with "On the Social Compact" (*SC*, I.6). There Rousseau poses the challenge that we need to find a form of association in such a way that each member "obeys only himself and remains as free as before" (*SC*, I.6.172). If we read this phrase as two related clauses meant to explain one another, then it seems that "freedom" is defined positively in terms of "obeying" only oneself in some manner, such as through self-legislation, and negatively by not being subject to the will of another. In turn, the following chapter, "On the Sovereign" (*SC*, I.7),

---

[16] See O'Hagan, *Rousseau* , 96–101; N. J. H. Dent, *Rousseau* (London: Basil Blackwell, 1988), 193–200; David Lay Williams, *Rousseau's* Social Contract*: An Introduction* (Cambridge: Cambridge University Press, 2014), 60. Masters also argues that "moral freedom" rests on the dualist metaphysics of the "Profession," but concludes that Rousseau does not insist upon that metaphysical commitment but makes it "detachable" (*Political Philosophy of Rousseau*, 73).

[17] Notably Ernst Cassirer, *The Question of Jean-Jacques Rousseau*, 1932, trans. and ed. Peter Gay, 2nd ed. (New Haven: Yale University Press, 1989). Matthew Simpson argues that moral freedom in Rousseau centers on autonomy, but he pushes back against Kantian readings. See "Moral Freedom", chap. 5 in *Rousseau's Theory of Freedom* (London: Continuum, 2006).

discusses the "double relationship" each associate has as both a member of the sovereign, who legislates, and a subject, who obeys the laws. What happens if an associate wants to make laws but not obey them? This is the occasion for Rousseau's infamous declaration that such a person must be "forced to be free," restoring the mutual engagement he has made with the other associates to act as both sovereign and subject (*SC*, I.7.174–75). In this way, the individual citizen is free, and forced to be so, by requiring self-legislation in such a way that it binds the individual considered as subject to the laws. This brings us to the chapter "On the Civil State."

"This transition from the state of nature to the civil state produces a very remarkable change in man, by substituting justice for instinct in his conduct and by giving his actions the morality they previously lacked," he begins the chapter. Here Rousseau's use of the term "morality" (*moralité*) is an instance of "moral" in the narrow sense of the term. He explains: "only then, when the voice of duty replaces physical impulse and right replaces appetite, does man, who until then had considered only himself, see himself forced to act on the basis of other principles and to consult his reason before listening to his inclinations." Rousseau often writes using binary terms, and he does so here. On the one side are instinct, physical impulse, appetite, and inclinations. On the other are justice, duty, right, and reason. The first set concerns what might be termed "physical" phenomena and the second set "moral" phenomena. Rousseau elaborates the advantages man gains from moving from the state of nature to the civil state: "his faculties exercised and developed, his ideas enlarged, his feelings ennobled, his entire soul so greatly elevated," and "from a stupid and limited animal, made an intelligent being and a man" (*SC*, I.8.175–76). This passage recalls the discussion in the *Discourse on Inequality* of man "from the metaphysical and moral side."

"Physical man" in the pure state of nature is a "stupid and limited animal," but he has the potential from perfectibility to become "an intelligent being and a man." Entering the civil state is the route (or at least a route) for effecting or completing this transformation.

Rousseau compares the losses and gains of leaving the natural state and entering the civil state in terms of a comparison between two forms of freedom: natural and civil. Natural freedom is "an unlimited right to everything that tempts him and that he can get." This form of freedom is related to the first set of binary terms discussed above: instinct, physical impulse, appetite, and inclinations. But it is now framed in terms of right and freedom: natural man has a right to exercise his freedom as he chooses. This is a form of self-legislation, although one tied to a greater or lesser extent to impulse, appetite, and inclination, and therefore not a fully self-conscious or rational form of freedom. In turn, what man gains in entering the civil state is civil freedom. Whereas natural freedom is bounded by the individual's force or power, "what he can get," civil freedom is "limited by the general will" (*SC*, I.8.176).

What is "civil freedom"? Some interpreters have suggested that civil freedom is the exercise of various activities, such as freedom of association, which are left to the citizens outside of the laws legislated by the general will.[18] I do not believe this is correct. If natural freedom is exercised by the individual through his particular will as an individual, and thus one form of self-legislation, then civil freedom would seem to be the exercise of the individual through his general will as a citizen, and thus another form of self-legislation, collective self-legislation. What is left to the citizen outside of the bounds of the general will, such as freedom of

[18] See Williams, *Rousseau's* Social Contract, 59–60.

association, would appear to be a form of natural freedom. In a later chapter, Rousseau explains: "it is acknowledged that through the social compact that each person alienates only that portion of the entirety of his power, his goods, and his freedom the use of which matters to the community, but it must also be acknowledged that the sovereign alone is judge of what matters" (*SC*, II.4.184). If so, then civil freedom is the form of self-legislation exercised through the general will one has as a citizen and which binds the citizen considered as subject.

Now we reach the third form of freedom: "moral freedom." Let me quote the entire brief paragraph:

> To the foregoing acquisitions of the civil state might be added moral freedom, which alone makes man truly the master of himself. For the impulsion of appetite alone is slavery, and obedience to the law one has prescribed to oneself is freedom. But I have already said too much about this topic, and the philosophical meaning of the word *freedom* is not my subject here. (*SC*, I.8.176)

This passage raises a number of interpretive questions.

First, the term itself: "moral freedom," *liberté morale*. I have determined that it is very nearly Rousseau's neologism. Searches of databases such as ARTFL[19] reveal only a few uses of the term before the *Social Contract*, and no systematic usage. The same is true for Latin, and for example the term *libertas moralis* occurs only once in Suarez. In turn, after the French Revolution the term becomes quite common, often with reference to Rousseau, for example in Mme de Staël. As for Rousseau, the term does not occur anywhere else in his published writings. The only other

[19] The ARTFL Project, Department of Romance Languages and Literatures, Division of the Humanities, University of Chicago, https://artfl-project.uchicago.edu/.

occurrence comes in a manuscript version of a note he added to the "Profession" in his role as editor, a passage which did not make its way to the final version.[20] In short, in order to comprehend what Rousseau means by "moral freedom" in the *Social Contract* all we have is what he writes in the passage quoted.

Second, what if anything does "moral freedom" add to "civil freedom"? Rousseau explains: "for the impulsion of appetite alone is slavery, and obedience to the law one has prescribed to oneself is freedom." This seems to be precisely what he has already said is gained by entering the civil state, especially if civil freedom is conceived as the collective form of self-legislation, as I have argued. What if we read this passage phenomenologically? In other words, what distinguishes civil freedom from natural freedom is the recognition, consciousness, and feeling of acting freely, and Rousseau terms this "moral freedom." If this is correct, then "moral freedom" is not so much a separate form of freedom than a different way of conceptualizing or describing the freedom we enjoy upon entering civil society and becoming fully human. This form of freedom involves the second set of binaries discussed above which describe the principles by which man acts upon entering the civil state: justice, duty, right, and reason. In short, a phenomenological reading of "moral freedom" entails no metaphysical commitments beyond a description of our experience.

Third, then what does Rousseau mean when he concludes the passage by stating: "but I have already said too much about this topic, and the philosophical meaning of the word *freedom* is not my subject here"? Where has Rousseau said "too much" about this topic, especially given that he never in fact says anything about "moral freedom" elsewhere in his writings? Some interpreters assume he refers to what he has said in the "Profession."[21]

---

[20] See Rousseau, *Emile*, in *Œuvres completes*, 4:586, var. *d*.

[21] See Masters, *Political Philosophy of Rousseau*, 73.

Since he does not discuss "moral freedom" there, and also since it is not Rousseau himself who speaks in the "Profession," about freedom or otherwise, this is not a satisfying interpretation. I suggest that he means that he has already said "too much" about the topic in this brief passage in the *Social Contract*, since the "philosophical meaning of the word *freedom*" is not his subject in his political treatise. What of the "philosophical" meaning of the term? Here we have another example of Rousseau intentionally sidestepping the issue of any metaphysical explanation of freedom, here "metaphysical" in the narrow sense of questions about materialism and dualism, etc. If a phenomenological understanding of freedom suffices to explain our experience, then Rousseau stops there.

Conclusion

I have argued that freedom in Rousseau's writings is best understood in phenomenological rather than metaphysical terms. Let me conclude with a confession. In using the term "metaphysical" to designate a certain interpretation of Rousseau's conception of freedom and human nature more generally, I have been using the term in the narrow sense I have identified, namely the area of philosophy dealing with questions of ontology, substance, etc., and especially issues concerning free will. Further, I might be accused of using the term as though it were synonymous with dualist metaphysics, for I am opposing interpretations of Rousseau that argue that a dualist metaphysics undergirds his understanding of freedom. My confession is that in my view Rousseau does in fact have a position on metaphysical questions, a position he does not develop explicitly or in those terms. As we saw when examining *Emile*, he reminds himself—and the reader—that he is not producing "a treatise on metaphysics and morals." Yet he is in fact doing just that, and in two ways. First, he is at minimum presenting a "metaphysical" treatise in the broad sense of the term, namely an account of the development and operation of the human mind: senses, ideas, judgment, and also sentiments or feelings. Second, I suggest that such an endeavor also entails or implies a "metaphysics" in the narrow sense of the term, namely what I would characterize as a non-reductionist materialism or, at any rate, a non-dualist theory. Such an argument will have to wait for another occasion. What I want to emphasize here is that Rousseau's conception of freedom is best understood in terms of our experience of freedom.

2.

THE PHILOSOPHER AS NATURAL MAN

Laurence D. Cooper

Ici repose l'homme de la nature et de la verité. One hesitates to allow others to speak for Rousseau, but these words, selected as an epitaph for Rousseau's tomb by his friend the Marquis Girardin,[1] speak what may be the most important truths about Rousseau, including the improbable truth that one could be, that *anyone* could be, both a man of nature and a man of truth in the ways that Rousseau understood himself to be—which is to say, as philosopher. Readers of the *Discourse on Inequality* have learned from Rousseau to equate nature with primordial origins. The natural man was a veritable brute who reasoned no more than other animals. Indeed, Rousseau presents reason not only as un- but as *anti*natural. The servant of interest, reason specializes in drowning out natural sentiment. And what is true of reason as such is all the more true of philosophy and the life thereof:

> it is by means of philosophy that [man] secretly says at the sight of a suffering man, perish if you wish, I am safe. Only dangers that threaten the entire society still

[1] See Maurice Cranston, *The Solitary Self: Jean-Jacques in Exile and Adversity* (Chicago: The University of Chicago Press, 1999), 188. Sixteen years later Rousseau's remains would be disinterred from their original resting place on the bucolic Isle of Poplars and moved with great fanfare to the Pantheon—where, however, the original epitaph can still be read.

> disturb the philosopher's tranquil slumber, and rouse him from his bed. One of his kind can with impunity be murdered beneath his window; he only has to put his hands over his ears and to argue with himself a little in order to prevent nature, which rebels within him, from letting him identify with the man being assassinated. (*SD*, 157)[2]

The smothering of natural sentiment is only the first of the evils Rousseau attributes to reason in general and philosophy in particular. Reason and philosophy not only undermine goodness by making us deaf to natural sentiment, they also undermine virtue and the religious and civil beliefs that undergird it. This, of course, had been the main thrust of the prior *Discourse on the Sciences and Arts*. To be sure, Rousseau vindicates reason and study in *Emile*, where their robust development is integral to the education and happiness of the "natural man living in the state of society" (*E*, 205).[3] But this education is shown to be impractical in the extreme; and not even in *Emile* does Rousseau ease up on philosophers. There too, as in the *Discourses*, philosophers are made out to be alienated from and subversive of goodness: "distrust those cosmopolitans who go to great length in their books to discover duties they do not deign to fulfill around them. A philosopher loves the Tartars so as to be spared having to love his neighbors" (*E*, 39). There too philosophers are shown to subvert virtue by undermining the beliefs and commitments that support it: like doctors and priests, philosophers "debase [man's]

[2] *SD*, cited by page number, will here refer to: *Second Discourse* or *Discourse on the Origin and the Foundations of Inequality Among Men*, trans. and ed. Victor Gourevitch in *Rousseau: The Discourses and Other Early Political Writings* (New York: Cambridge University Press, 2019).

[3] *E*, cited by page number, will refer to: *Emile, or on Education*, trans. Allan Bloom (New York: Basic Books, 1979).

heart and make him unlearn how to die" (*E*, 55). And there too Rousseau calls out philosophers for their bad faith and challenges them on their greatest point of pride. He knows of no other station with as many *prejudices* as philosophy (*E*, 243).

And yet Rousseau's critique of philosophy and philosophers isn't quite wholesale. Even amid his most excoriating attacks, he allows for exceptions. In the *First Discourse* he pointedly exempts a few great thinkers and even suggests that they be offered positions of influence in the courts of kings (*FD*, 28).[4] In the *Second Discourse* he submits his argument concerning the unnaturalness and inhumanity of philosophers to the judgment of the likes of Plato and Xenocrates (*SD*, 136). And in *Emile* he praises philosophers like Plato and Pythagoras for being unblinded by interest and prejudice—for knowing, in effect, how to see (*E*, 454). Rousseau's critique of philosophy is largely a critique of *popularized* philosophy, and most of the philosophers (*les philosophes*) whom he denigrates are best thought of as pretenders or false philosophers. He does admire "*true* philosophers" (*Preface*, 104; emphasis added),[5] but only rarely does that phrase denote great minds. Far more often it designates men of *moral* probity, as it memorably does in the conclusion of the *First Discourse* (*FD*, 27–28). When Rousseau explicitly refers to someone as a philosopher, it is almost always in a critical vein, whereas when he singles out a Plato or Socrates or Bacon or Descartes for praise, he normally refrains from referring to them as philosophers, preferring

[4] *FD*, cited by page number, will refer to: *First Discourse* or *Discourse on the Sciences and Arts*, trans. Victor Gourevitch in *Rousseau: The Discourses and Other Early Political Writings*.

[5] *Preface*, cited by page number, will refer to: *Preface to Narcissus*, trans. Victor Gourevtich in *Rousseau: The Discourses and Other Early Political Writings*.

instead to refer to them as "celestial intelligences," "sublime geniuses," or "preceptors of the human race."[6]

Yet even if he allows that certain philosophers are praiseworthy, Rousseau never says that philosophy or the philosophic life is in any way grounded in *nature*—neither when praising a philosopher nor when speaking of a natural man. Those philosophers whom he singles out for praise could certainly be said to be less encumbered than others by unnatural desires and prejudices, but that is not the same thing as saying that philosophizing is natural. And none of those whom he refers to as a natural man is a philosopher. The savage of the state of nature as depicted in the *Second Discourse* would have had no inkling of philosophy. And the "natural man living in the state of society," though curious and even animated by an "ardor to know," is interested only in knowledge connected to his interests, not knowledge of the whole or knowledge for its own sake (*E*, 167). There is yet one more natural man in Rousseau's corpus, of course, and that is Rousseau himself. Despite suffering peculiarly unnatural conditions early in life, with the predictable result that he would suffer his share or more than his share of unnatural passions, Rousseau depicts himself as somehow having preserved his natural goodness to an exceptional degree and even as having made a kind of return to nature.[7] He was able to initiate this return upon discovering the principle of natural goodness and thinking through its implications—which is to say, by, or at least with the necessary assistance of, philosophy. Yet even if his philosophizing was in

[6] See, for example, *Preface*, 104; *Final Reply of J.-J. Rousseau of Geneva*, 65; and *FD* 27–28, in *Rousseau: The Discourses and Other Early Political Writings*.

[7] Christopher Kelly has persuasively demonstrated that the story Rousseau tells in the *Confessions* is the story of an admittedly partial but still extraordinary return to nature. See Kelly, *Rousseau's Exemplary Life: The "Confessions" as Political Philosophy* (Ithaca, NY: Cornell University Press, 1987).

the service of nature, Rousseau still does not depict philosophy as natural in any deeper or intrinsic sense. And he does not depict himself as naturally given to philosophizing. Far from it. Nature expresses itself in inclinations or dispositions. We are drawn to what is natural, or at least to what is attractive to our own particular nature (*naturel*), by the implicit promise of pleasure, suitability, or happiness (*E*, 39). But Rousseau disavows precisely this experience of philosophy. Reviewing his life in his final work, *The Reveries of the Solitary Walker*, he recounts that although he sometimes thought deeply, "thinking was always a painful and charmless occupation" for him (*R*, 91).[8] And so we have it: the philosopher is no natural man, and the natural man philosophizes only in order to attain a condition wherein he needn't philosophize any more. Philosophy might serve nature, but it is not an intrinsically natural pursuit. Rousseau would never see fit to qualify the sweeping judgment he pronounced in the *Second Discourse*: "if [nature] destined us to be healthy then, I almost dare assert, the state of reflection is a state against nature, and the man who meditates a depraved animal" (*SD*, 141).

As it happens, though, he didn't need to qualify this statement, for it was already qualified: "I *almost* dare assert—." Is reflection *not* against nature, then—not always? Might it be against nature only when, say, pursued for the sake of certain ends, such as reputation? In fact, this proves to be Rousseau's view. A natural man might be a philosopher. Rousseau the natural man *was* a philosopher; and he was so, if I may say so, *by nature*, not only in the sense that the life of philosophy suited and expressed his particular nature (his *naturel*) but that it belongs to and expresses

[8] *R*, cited by page number, will refer to: *The Reveries of the Solitary Walker*, trans. Charles E. Butterworth (Indianapolis: Hackett Publishing Company, 1992).

human nature as such. To explain how the philosophic life can be regarded as a natural life and the philosopher as a natural man—indeed, the *most* natural man—will require that we take careful note of what Rousseau says and doesn't say about nature. In particular we will need to attend carefully to the distinction between *description*, no matter how compelling or seemingly universal, and *definition*. But before we undertake that task, we need to work through an obstacle that we've already met—namely, the apparent disavowal of philosophy embodied in Rousseau's claim to dislike thinking. This statement too is qualified. What appears to be a claim to dislike thinking as such proves upon careful examination to apply only to one kind of thinking. Other kinds of thinking are effectively celebrated as pleasant—not just reverie but also various kinds of rigorous, discursive, and even scientific thinking. Indeed, in my view the *Reveries* as a whole proves to be an articulation of and apologia for the philosophic life understood as a life of radical, unending inquiry.[9]

Let's look at the whole of Rousseau's seeming disavowal of philosophy:

---

[9] I have made the case for the *Reveries* as Rousseau's articulation of and apologia for the philosophic life in *Dreaming of Justice, Waking to Wisdom: Rousseau's Philosophic Life* (Chicago: The University of Chicago Press, 2023). I also argue there that the *Reveries* tells the *story* of Rousseau's philosophic life and thus to some extent the story of the philosophic life as such in its coming-to-be, its being, and its further perfection. Few interpreters have recognized that the *Reveries* is an exploration of the philosophic life. And of those who have, none to my knowledge has read the book as a story of a (or the) philosophic life. See Heinrich Meier, *On the Happiness of the Philosophic Life: Reflections on Rousseau's "Rêveries,"* trans. Robert Berman (Chicago: University of Chicago Press, 2016); Michael Davis, *The Autobiography of Philosophy: Rousseau's* The Reveries of the Solitary Walker (Lanham, MD: Rowman and Littlefield, 1999); and Victor Gourevitch, "A Provisional Reading of Rousseau's *Reveries of the Solitary Walker*," *Review of Politics* 74, no. 3 (Summer 2012): 489–518.

> I have sometimes thought rather deeply, but rarely with pleasure, almost always against my liking, and as though by force. Reverie relaxes and amuses me; reflection tires and saddens me; thinking always was a painful and charmless occupation for me. Sometimes my reveries end in meditation, but more often my meditations end in reverie; and during these wanderings, my soul rambles and glides through the universe on the wings of imagination, in ecstasies which surpass every other enjoyment. (*R*, 91)

This passage appears amid a lengthy discussion of botany, wherein Rousseau contrasts his way of botanizing with that of others. Whereas others practice botany instrumentally, for medicinal purposes, he delights in the study of plants for the wonders that they *are*. And this delight, he gives us to understand, goes under the name of reverie. It does not take long, however, for the reader to realize that however Rousseau has chosen to label it, botany as he pursues it is rigorously scientific. His botanizing presupposes considerable knowledge and understanding, and it yields more of the same. And in the very next paragraph Rousseau reports that his reveries had previously languished and cooled and were only very rarely within reach (*R*, 91). Botany as he has come to practice it is not a reverie-based practice at all. Is it a thinking practice? Rousseau's account of how he came to botanize the way that he does suggests that it is. As he tells the story, a certain self-protective "instinct imposed silence upon my imagination and, fixing my attention upon the objects which surrounded me, made me consider in detail for the first time the spectacle of nature which until then I had hardly contemplated except in a mass and all together [*dans son ensemble*]" (*R*, 91).[10]

[10] I have departed from Butterworth's translation at the end of this line. He renders *dans son ensemble* as "in its wholeness," whereas Rousseau's point

Made me consider in detail—this begins to sound like science. Indeed, Rousseau almost immediately begins to speak of apprehending nature as a *system*, and there can be no apprehending a system except through analytic thinking. He recounts ecstatic and transcendent experiences of losing himself in or blending into this system. There are two such passages. In the first, he speaks not just of himself but of anyone who knows how to look at nature; hence the third-person voice: "A sweet and deep reverie takes possession of his senses then, and through a delicious intoxication he loses himself in the immensity of this beautiful system with which he feels himself one" (*R*, 92). The second passage appears seven paragraphs later; it is cast in the first person: "I feel ecstasies and inexpressible raptures in blending, so to speak, into the system of beings and in making myself one with the whole of nature [*la nature entire*]" (*R*, 95). The ecstatic experience of transcendence, however "mystical" it may sound, depends on scientific analysis. This dependence, moreover, is not only developmental but phenomenological and ongoing: Rousseau's oneness with nature requires not only that he *have* apprehended nature as a system but also that he *continue* to apprehend it that way, which is to say, that he continue to *think*, that he continue to hold in mind the *articulation* of nature as system, even as he *reflects* on the experiences that he has recounted.

In the three paragraphs that separate these two accounts of his ecstatic oneness with nature, Rousseau contrasts his own way of and reasons for botanizing with the ways and reasons of almost every other botanist. (As we have begun to see, botany pretty clearly stands in for the study of nature as such, or philosophy.) In this brief compass he lets us see that, however much he may tire at some kinds of thinking, he *loves* other kinds, and he

---

here, it seems to me, is to highlight that to contemplate something in a mass is to *fail* to see wholeness.

gradually reveals what is at issue between the two categories of thought. *He* gives himself up to "delicious impressions of surrounding objects" (*R*, 92). *They* investigate plants with a practical purpose that has nothing to do with immediate enjoyment, whether sensory or otherwise. *His* eyes roam from one object to another across a great variety of sights and always light upon something captivating. *Their* eyes do their seeing through microscopes; they look upon nature only in order to determine which specimens to bring back to the lab. *He* delights in "ocular recreation," drawing great pleasure from "fragrant odors, intense colors, [and] the most elegant shapes," which compete with one another to present themselves to him. *They* do not. Rousseau explains why this might be:

> To give oneself up to such delicious sensations, it is necessary only to love pleasure. And if this effect does not occur for all those who perceive these objects, with some it is due to a lack of natural sensitivity and with most it is because their mind, too preoccupied with other ideas, only furtively gives itself up to the objects which strike their senses.

Yet another thing contributes to turning refined people's attention away from the vegetable realm: the habit of seeking only drugs and remedies in plants (*R*, 92–93).

Those who study plants only in search of remedies do not truly see plants at all: "medicine has taken possession of plants and transformed them into simples to such an extent that *we see in them what we do not see in them at all*, to wit, the pretended virtues it pleases just anybody to attribute to them" (*R*, 93; emphasis added). Rousseau does not eschew all botany that is undertaken for instrumental reasons. He notes with pleasure that he has "often thought that the vegetable realm was a storehouse of foods given to man and animals by nature" (*R*, 94), and he praises Linnaeus for "somewhat tak[ing] botany out of pharmacology schools and [bringing] it back to natural history and economic uses" (*R*, 93). What offends him is thinking that is instrumental in a certain *way*, or for one particular reason:

> This turn of mind, which always brings everything back to our material interest, which causes us to seek profit or remedies everywhere, and which would cause us to regard all of nature with indifference if we were always well, has never been mine. With respect to that, I feel just the opposite of other men: *everything which pertains to feeling my needs saddens and spoils my thoughts, and I have never found true charm in the pleasures of my mind except when concern for my body was completely lost from sight* (*R*, 94; emphasis added).

What Rousseau dislikes is not thinking as such but thinking that arises from concern for the body. It is important to note that what *arises from* concern for the body includes more than the body itself. It includes the self which, being vested in the body, understands itself to be separate from and vulnerable to others and thus locked in competition with them. This is the self insofar as it is governed or constituted by amour-propre, the relative form of self-love that tends to supersede absolute self-love, or *amour de soi*. Consciousness of the needs of this self is burdensome because it makes us feel our vulnerability and dependence—which tends to intensify our felt vulnerability and dependence all the more. In short, the thinking that Rousseau dislikes is the thinking of an insecure amour-propre. And amour-propre is never *not* insecure. Not that *amour de soi* is indifferent to one's well-being, but, unlike amour-propre, it is not invested in such radically contingent and embattled "needs" as status and it does not resist necessity (including mortality) on the purported grounds of justice. *Amour de soi*, or the self to the extent that it is governed by *amour de soi*, will accept what it needs to accept, if only because it knows that not accepting the necessary and inevitable will only make for more unhappiness.

We now approach the heart of the matter. Recall that Rousseau took up his new way of botanizing when a certain self-protective "instinct" silenced his imagination (*R*, 91). What was this instinct protecting him *against*? His answer is quite illuminating. He needed to quiet his imagination, he tells us, "lest the continual sentiment of [his] troubles, gradually *constricting* [his] heart, crush [him] at last with its weight" (emphasis added). The vocabulary of constriction and expansion, though used sparingly in the *Reveries*, is enormously revealing. "Being," in Rousseau's view—by which I mean, following his usage, the *sentiment* of being—is the very stuff and measure of life. This being or feeling of being comes by doing, or by exercising one's faculties, including intellectual faculties. Thinking that arises from the neediness of amour-propre will always tend to constrict one's being.[11]

Yet if some kinds of thinking constrict one's being, other kinds might *expand* it. Rather than wearying, thinking can be enthralling—as it is for Rousseau: "no, nothing personal, nothing which concerns my body can truly occupy my soul. I never meditate, I never dream more deliciously [*Je médite, je ne rêve jamais plus délicieusement*] than when I forget myself. I feel ecstasies and inexpressible raptures in blending, so to speak, into the system of beings and in making myself one with the whole of nature" (*R*, 95). When I called attention to this passage above it was to point

[11] Regarding constriction and expansion in Rousseau's thought generally, see my "Between Eros and Will to Power," *American Political Science Review* 98, no. 1 (February 2004): 105–19; or "Rousseau and the Expansiveness of Being," part 2 of *Eros in Plato, Rousseau, and Nietzsche: The Politics of Infinity* (University Park: The Pennsylvania State University Press, 2008). For further explication of the ways in which thinking in particular might or might not contribute to the extension of one's being, see *Eros*, 155–69.

out that Rousseau's "reveries," at least some of them, consist in rigorous and scientific thought; this was implied by his focus on *system*. Now I'd like to call attention to a different element of Rousseau's experience. Namely, in blending into the system of nature he was making himself one with the *whole* of nature. *He extended his being indefinitely*—and without the anxiety and self-vacating that follows from trying to extend one's being through possessing wealth, power, or status, which is the way of amour-propre. One might wonder whether what Rousseau is describing here truly merits being called thinking. And Rousseau of course doesn't call it thinking (*penser*). But let's look at what he does call it. To *meditate* (*méditer*), as Rousseau uses the word and its cognates in the *Reveries*, always encompasses reflection. And while *dreaming* admittedly connotes something less than rigorous thinking, the connotation is often misleading in Rousseau's case, since he used this term and its cognates, especially *rêverie*, to refer to a broad array of cognitive activities—not only dreaming or daydreaming but also rigorous reflection.[12] (As Rousseau applies the word "reverie" to a broad array of cognitive activities, so he applies the word "thinking" to a remarkably narrow range of activity.)[13] *The Reveries of the Solitary Walker* is hardly the first of

[12] Meier observes that in each of the three Walks in which "reverie" seems to designate an activity, the activity is one or another kind of rigorous thinking: "by means of replacement and delimitation, *rêverie* is more precisely determined to be *réflexion*, *meditation*, and *contemplation*." But these more rigorous activities have something in common with reverie: each "is characterized as essentially free of social constraint or any purpose external to them." In short, the word "reveries" "serves Rousseau as a sign-post to the philosophic activity of the *Promeneur Solitaire* and as its abbreviation." H. Meier, "Roussseau and the Philosophic Life," in T. Burns, ed. *Recovering Reason* (Lanham: Lexington Books, 2020), 315.

[13] Concerning Rousseau's strangely narrow use of the word "thinking" in the Seventh Walk, see Victor Gourevitch, "A Provisional Reading of Rousseau's *Reveries of the Solitary Walker*," *The Review of Politics* 74, no. 3 (Summer 2012): 489–518. Gourevitch observes that Rousseau "would seem here to reserve 'thinking' primarily for practical or instrumental thinking, doing and

his books in which Rousseau used the word "reverie" to refer to rigorous, sophisticated, and philosophic reflection. In the *First Discourse*, he commented on "the dangerous reveries of such men as Hobbes and Spinoza" (*FD*, 27–28; 20), and in a letter to Voltaire he referred to the *Second Discourse* as his own "sad reveries."[14] Nor was Rousseau's peculiar use of the word as peculiar as all that. Montaigne and Descartes had used the word to encompass philosophic reflection, as did Diderot.[15] Why Rousseau chose to speak this way is perhaps not so difficult to figure out. In an age of corrupt refinement and popularized or pseudo-philosophy, phenomena that subvert both goodness and virtue (that is, *natural* goodness and *civic* virtue) and indeed philosophy itself, he wanted to avoid burnishing the appeal of intellectual pursuits and promote instead the innocent, rustic, pleasures, the *natural* pleasures, of the country. And if his designating these experiences

---

making, in contrast to 'revery' which he would seem here to reserve primarily for thinking for its own sake alone, with no determinate end or aim beyond itself. The contrast between them would seem to correspond to the distinction between travail and amusement. They differ not so much in what one is thinking about as in how and why one thinks about it. The objects of 'thinking' and 'revery'—God, freedom, immortality, duty, happiness, persecution—may be the same, but how and with what end in view one is thinking about them differ; and so therefore may what may be said about them" (508).

[14] See Gourevitch, "Provisional Reading," 489–90n1. Gourevitch's brief gloss makes the central point: "the term traditionally makes what is being said appear more innocuous than it is." Also see Meier, *Happiness*, 132 and 14: the fact that "few readers will connect serious and profound meditation with the designation *reverie*" allows Rousseau to use the word "both to point to and to divert attention away from the activity central to the philosophic life."

[15] See Marcel Raymond, "Introduction" to the *Reveries*, in Rousseau, *Œuvres complètes*, ed. Bernard Gagnebin and Marcel Raymond, 5 vols. (Paris: Gallimard, Bibliothèque de la Pléiade, 1959–95), lxxxvi-lxxxviii. Raymond additionally notes that one M. Sorbiere, mid-seventeenth-century translator into French of Hobbes's *De cive*, spoke admiringly (in his own name) of "the reveries of Hobbes, Gassendi and Descartes."

"reveries" does not count against the scientific character of the activities, neither does his professed "self-forgetting," for he never does forget himself. He never ceases to be aware of his experience as his own. He does forget something about himself—but what? In feeling himself one with nature, he ceases to experience—he "forgets"—only his separateness from nature. To forget one's separateness from nature is to forget only a certain form of the self (as Plato might put it), namely, the self insofar as it is constituted by amour-propre. What's more, with this forgetting of one form of self comes the recovery of another form of self, a prior, natural self, the self that is constituted by *amour de soi*. The recovery of the natural self with its clearer sight makes possible a *more perfect* science and philosophy.

Finally, it bears noting that Rousseau's claim to dislike thinking is stated with respect to thinking considered as an *occupation* (*penser fut toujours pour moi une <u>occupation</u> pénible et sans charme*). "Occupation" suggests activity that one has contracted to do, meaning activity that one is now obliged to do. And Rousseau had already said in the Sixth Walk that even the most gratifying activity loses its charm for him once it has become an obligation (*R*, 75–76).

In sum, these qualifications are so extensive as to render Rousseau's apparent disavowal of philosophy an informed celebration of the philosophic life. And they are so artful as to go unnoticed by the vast majority of readers, who will thereby have shown themselves to be questionable candidates for the philosophic life.

***

Rousseau by contrast is well suited to the philosophic life, and he knows himself to be so. He also knows, or believes he knows, that philosophy and the philosophic life are *natural*—and not only for him or with respect to his particular *naturel* but for human beings as such, even if most human beings lack the necessary preparation and probably the requisite *naturel.* Let us now look directly into Rousseau's view of nature and naturalness in human beings—not so much how he depicts or describes it but how he defines it.

Rousseau equates the natural with the original (*le primitif*), just as most readers, including most scholars, suppose. These same readers, however, go too far—or rather, not far enough—in comprehending what this means. Following Rousseau's evident practice in the *Second Discourse*, they understand by "original" that which was *temporally* first. Yet "original" admits of other meanings. It can refer to logical or ontological primacy, to the essence or the actuating principle, or, better yet, the form of a thing, i.e., that on account of which it is the kind of thing that it is, as is the case in Plato and Aristotle, who frequently use the word (*archē*) this way,[16] sometimes in overt opposition to those who limit the word's meaning to temporal origins. Plato and Aristotle were explicit about the way they used the term. Rousseau is not. But he is clear all the same—in the only definition of nature to be found in his corpus:

> We are born with the use of our senses, and from our birth we are affected in various ways by the objects surrounding us. As soon as we have, so to speak, consciousness of our sensations, we are disposed to seek or avoid the objects which produce them, at first according to whether they are pleasant or unpleasant to us, then according to the conformity or lack of it that we find between us and these objects, and finally according to the

[16] For instances of *archē* employed in a non-temporal sense see, for example, *The Republic of Plato*, trans. Allan Bloom (New York: Basic Books, 1991), 511b; *Phaedrus*, trans. James H. Nichols (Ithaca, NY: Cornell University Press, 1998), 245c–d; and book 5 of *Aristotle's Metaphysics*, trans. Joe Sachs (Santa Fe: Green Lion Press, 2002).

> judgments we make about them on the basis of the idea of happiness or of perfection given us by reason. These dispositions are extended and strengthened as we become more capable of using our senses and more enlightened; but constrained by our habits, they are more or less corrupted by our opinions. Before this corruption they are what I call in us *nature*. (*E*, 39; emphasis in the original)

What is natural in human beings, as Rousseau puts it in the sentence immediately following the passage I've just quoted, are our "*original* dispositions" (emphasis added), meaning dispositions that are not corrupt: dispositions that have *developed* but have not been corrupted; dispositions whose bases are sensory and *rational* ("judgments we make…on the basis of the idea of happiness or of perfection given us by *reason*"). Reason is part of human beings' natural endowment, and reason that remains uncorrupted contributes to the increased perfection of nature.[17] Yes, nature *can be* perfected. There are two elements or metrics implicit in Rousseau's definition of the natural. One is negative: nature as lack of corruption. This is the dimension that predominates almost entirely in the *Second Discourse*. The other is positive and teleological: nature as the development or perfection of our innate capacities and dispositions. In a crucial sense the negative criterion trumps the positive one, and not only in the telling of the *Second Discourse*: that which has developed but has been corrupted is not natural. But the negative criterion does not obviate the positive one: uncorrupted capacities and dispositions that are

---

[17] The *Dialogues* too allows for the naturalness of reason. See, *Rousseau, Judge of Jean-Jacques: Dialogues*, trans. Judith R. Bush, Christopher Kelly, and Roger D. Masters, in *The Collected Writings of Rousseau*, eds. Roger D. Masters and Christopher Kelly (Hanover, NH: University Press of New England, 1990), 1:214. Hereafter cited as *D*, by page number.

highly developed are preferable to and more natural than uncorrupted capacities and dispositions that have not been highly developed. They are *preferable* because they afford the person at issue a fuller life or a more deeply experienced sentiment of being. They are *more natural* first, because there is a given direction or pathway that, if followed, would lead them to be more fully what they are, and, second, because this direction or pathway *would* be followed if corrupting influences didn't intervene. (This applies to capacities and dispositions that lay dormant in primeval times.) In *Emile*, Rousseau speaks of nature's "goal" (*E*, 38) and he refers in numerous places to the "march," "path," or "order" either of nature as such or of the faculties or passions that belong to our nature (*E*, 34, 47, 219–20). He characterizes the education he gives to his imagined pupil Emile, an education that develops the lad's reason and sensibilities to the utmost extent that ordinary human nature will allow, as "the education of nature" (*E*, 41). And he refers to the man who emerges from that education as "the natural man living in the state of society" (*E*, 205). There is no reason to regard Emile's naturalness as qualified or metaphorical, so long as he has become all that ordinary human nature allows. Finally, on the basis of Rousseau's definition of nature—again, the only definition he offers—a person with extraordinary natural gifts who has avoided or overcome corruption should be considered still more natural, or better yet, more perfectly natural, even than Emile. Rousseau is such a one himself. And there's no knowing that nature wouldn't allow for something or someone even more perfectly natural than he: "we do not know what our nature permits us to be" (*E*, 62).

This last remark from *Emile* might seem to argue against considering Rousseau's understanding of nature to be teleological. Doesn't teleology require a fixed telos? But it seems to me that we can think of and aim even at an indefinite end, so long as we can specify the precise direction in which it lies, i.e., the principle that it instantiates. The end is the furthest possible progress in that precise direction.

There are other elements to Rousseau's conception of nature that might seem to undermine the case for regarding it as teleological; but these too, though they surely complicate the case, don't refute it. One such element is the disparity of natures (*naturels*) among human beings—not just with respect to dispositions but also with respect to innate capabilities. Nature has distributed physical, intellectual, and dispositional capacities and inclinations unevenly. Even strength of soul varies by nature among human beings. *Great* strength of soul, the decisive quality of all outstanding human beings, seems to be, or at least depend on, a rare natural endowment (*E*, 106). And nature sometimes badly *under*performs. In one instance Rousseau speaks of "nature's *mistakes*" (*E*, 199–200; emphasis added): the reference is to "those crowds of cowardly men whose heart it [nature] has mutilated." Other complicating elements include the enormous difficulty of knowing, let alone following, the order of nature in society and the challenging fact that in order to follow the order of nature one must somehow actively cultivate it while departing from inclination and even instinct (*E*, 254). Although "it is always from nature itself that the proper instruments to regulate nature must be drawn" (*E*, 327), this regulation will sometimes entail forgoing "the most natural expedient" (*E*, 317). Indeed, Rousseau counsels us to "distrust instinct as soon as you no longer limit yourself to it. It is good as long as it acts by itself; it is suspect from the moment it operates within man-made institutions. It must not be destroyed, but it must be regulated, and that is perhaps more difficult than annihilating it" (*E*, 333–34).[18] Even if nature has a single goal, the requisite means to that goal are inevitably affected by circumstance: "I will be told that I abandon nature. I do not believe that at all. It chooses its instruments and regulates them according to need, not to opinion. Now, needs change according to the situation of men. There is a great difference between the natural man living in the state of nature and the natural man living in the state of society" (*E*, 205). Again, these facts surely complicate the quest for nature, both the theoretical and the practical quest, but they do not obviate it. It is worth noting that each of the complications that I've just noted—each of the *principles* that give rise to these complications—is found in Aristotle as well. Nature is an end, Aristotle says, but he never says that all are equipped (or even, come to think of it, that *any* are equipped) to reach it. Aristotle famously proclaimed the city natural and man by nature a rational and political animal even though all cities inevitably fall far short of this end, including even the city with the best regime.[19] Nature is introduced in the *Politics* almost as a benevolent goddess. Benevolent she may be, but her intentions aren't always realized (*Politics*, 1254b).[20]

---

[18] "One must use a great deal of art to prevent social man from being totally artificial" (*E*, 317). Surely the needed art is the political art or the art of the legislator.

[19] The best regime as sketched in book 7 of the *Politics* includes slaves who do not come close to meeting the criteria of natural slaves as articulated in book 1.

[20] In the passage at issue Aristotle writes that nature wishes to assign different bodies to free persons and slaves but that this wish is often denied. With this observation Aristotle undermines an argument about slavery that he has seemed to be making. But he does not undermine the case for regarding nature as an end. What is natural is what is good for this or that species of natural being, not what is universal or even common. Consider book 1, chapter 2 of the *Politics*, trans. Carnes Lord (Chicago: University of Chicago Press, 1984). Immediately after declaring the city natural and the human being a

Benevolence doesn't always mean beneficence. And nature's demands, meaning the demands of natural right, vary as greatly as do the demands of conventional or positive right (*Nicomachean Ethics*, 1134b).[21]

Nature as an end is absent from the *Second Discourse*. Not *precluded*, I hasten to say, but absent. If we were to take the *Second Discourse*'s depiction of nature as a limiting *definition*, there could be no such thing as a "natural man living in the state of society" or a "savage made to inhabit cities" (*E*, 205), and the philosopher would be among the *least* natural human beings imaginable. And yet as I have noted, most readers do take the *Second Discourse*'s depiction of nature as a limiting definition.[22] That they do so should come as no great surprise, for Rousseau seems to have

---

rational and political animal, he praises the founder of the first city as a great benefactor: that we are naturally directed to an end doesn't mean that many or even any of us will attain it.

[21] *Nicomachean Ethics*, trans. Joe Sachs (Newburyport, MA: Focus Publishing, 2002).

[22] Some notable exceptions should be mentioned. See especially Jonathan Marks, *Perfection and Disharmony in the Thought of Jean-Jacques Rousseau* (New York: Cambridge University Press, 2005), who argues not only for Rousseau's nature as teleological but also against the naturalness of the denizen of the *Second Discourse*'s state of nature. Nevertheless there are two important differences between Marks's view and mine. First, whereas I see Rousseau equating nature with origins, albeit origins in a sense that supersedes temporality, Marks rejects the equation of nature and origins in Rousseau's thought tout court. Second, Marks seems to see Emile, who has an ordinary nature, as *the* exemplar of naturalness in Rousseau's thought, though he does seem to allow for the possibility that Rousseau might see one or another exceptional human being as the person who most fully approaches or realizes our natural telos. Others who resist regarding the *Second Discourse* as Rousseau's governing statement on nature include N. J. H. Dent, *Rousseau: An Introduction to his Psychological, Social, and Political Theory* (Oxford: Basil Blackwell, 1988); Jeffrey A. Smith, "Natural Happiness, Sensation, and Infancy in Rousseau's *Emile*," *Polity* 35, no. 1 (Fall 2002): 94–122; and Victor Gourevitch, "Rousseau's Pure State of Nature," *Interpretation* 16, no. 1 (Fall 1988): 23–59.

deliberately invited this (mis)understanding. In part 1 of the *Discourse* he describes in intricate detail the primitive being whom he explicitly calls "the natural man" and the condition of life in what he explicitly calls "the state of nature." And part 2's conjectural account of how and why civilized human beings have become what they are depicts a growing and seemingly irreversible alienation from nature. Why invite misunderstanding? The likeliest answer is a practical one that we've already discussed, namely, to avoid further burnishing the appeal of the sciences and arts and especially philosophy.[23]

Rousseau also seems to me to have had a powerful *theoretical* reason for exploring nature in the way he does in the *Second Discourse*. Sometimes one can give a uniquely incisive account of what *is* by telling a story, which may or may not be literally true, that purports to tell what once *was*. If Rousseau regards nature as an end, that end includes within itself structures and dispositions that temporally preceded it. What is natural in human beings are dispositions that have developed or grown, and there can be no complete understanding of growth without considering the growing itself and its stages. Rousseau recognized that a genetic account of nature could accomplish things that an eidetic account could not.[24] Our "present nature" (*SD*, 127), as unnatural as it is, still includes what belonged to our primeval ancestors.[25] And the

---

[23] For further reflection on why Rousseau would have wished to have most readers regard the *Second Discourse* as his decisive statement on nature even though it wasn't, see Marks, "Rousseau's Rhetorical Strategy," chap. 3 in *Perfection and Disharmony*.

[24] "'Eidetic' is short for what results from an analysis of something into its kinds, 'genetic' stands for the result of examining the coming into being of a genus or one genus from another." See Seth Benardete, *Plato's "Laws"* (Chicago: University of Chicago Press, 2000), 18n18.

[25] Can "man's present *nature*" really be in any way *un*natural? This is the place to cite Rousseau's important caveat about usage: "I have a hundred times

same development that humanity as a whole underwent over millennia is replicated in some way in the life of every individual. The prehistoric condition of humanity depicted in part 1 of the *Second Discourse* presents our "original dispositions" (*E*, 39) in their *temporally* original state. Part 2's conjectural history suggests how it happened that our original dispositions were "extended and strengthened" but also "corrupted"[26]—while also allowing, however quietly, the possibility of a better way.[27] A better way would be governance of the soul more in accord with *amour de soi*. The *best* way, because *most* in accord with and most fulfilling of *amour de soi*, would be the philosophic life.

***

Amour-propre is the source or stuff of the prejudices, delusions, and passions that corrupt us (*SD*, 189, 192–93, 202–4). Accordingly, the predominance of *amour de soi* over amour-propre in the soul is the most incontrovertible indication and measure of naturalness in a human being. The philosopher, the *true* philosopher, is the one who has overcome amour-propre most completely. The philosopher is not without amour-propre, nor would he want to be, for amour-propre is the source not only of the worst but also of the best things about us (*SD*, 189). In Rousseau's case, as perhaps in the case of any philosopher, amour-propre played a

in writing made the reflection that it is impossible in a long work always to give the same meanings to the same words. There is no language rich enough to furnish as many terms, turns, and phrases as our ideas can have modifications" (*E*, 108n).

[26] Michael Davis aptly observes that "it is a regular feature of Rousseau's writing to present what seem to be logical relations as temporal movements." See *The Music of Reason: Rousseau, Nietzsche, Plato* (Philadelphia: University of Pennsylvania Press, 2020), 16.

[27] See Heinrich Meier, "*The Discourse on the Origin and the Foundations of Inequality Among Men*: On the Intention of Rousseau's Most Philosophical Work," *Interpretation* 16, no. 2 (Winter 1988–89): 211–27.

part in impelling him first toward the philosophic life and then in it; this we can see in the *Confessions* and the *Reveries*.[28] And amour-propre is crucial to any number of worthwhile activities and experiences that, though not exclusive to the life of the philosopher, can certainly be part of it. The inevitable presence of amour-propre in the soul—and its presence *is* inevitable in socialized human beings (*E*, 215)—need not signify corruption, at least not in principle. Amour-propre can be tempered and even governed by reason that is in the service of *amour de soi*. (Amour-propre can also be governed by reason that is in the service of virtue and community, i.e., by the legislator's reason.) But the sovereignty of *amour de soi* in the soul signifies only the first of the two dimensions of naturalness in a human being. It signifies that one's "original dispositions" have not been corrupted, but it says nothing about the development or perfection of those dispositions. The case for the philosopher as a natural human being should speak directly to specifically human development. How so? We might argue that the philosopher is one in whom reason is most fully developed. And this would be a fully adequate response—if Rousseau, like Aristotle, contended that reason is the

[28] Rousseau like the rest of us lived a life full of convention and artifice; and he experienced his share of unnatural passions and probably more than his share of peculiar ones, owing to the co-presence in his soul of an exquisitely subtle and intelligent sensibility and an exceedingly touchy amour-propre. Yet we can discern from the *Reveries* and the *Confessions* that he had never succumbed entirely to amour-propre. Why Rousseau was able to resist being thoroughly overtaken by amour-propre is ultimately unknowable, but the proximate causes seem to have included both a rare nature and various encounters with benign individuals (including Madame de Warens and some discerning priests) who seemed to see something of this nature. For more on what sustained Rousseau's natural goodness or his access thereto and how this enabled him to embark on a more natural and philosophic life, see my "Nearer My True Self to Thee: Rousseau's Spirituality—and Ours," *The Review of Politics* 74, no. 3 (Summer 2012): 465–88.

distinctive and decisive human endowment. But he doesn't. Rousseau locates human distinctiveness not in reason but rather in freedom and the faculty of self-perfection (*SD*, 143–45; 214). Can a case for the philosopher's naturalness be made on those grounds? It can.

Since antiquity, advocates of the philosophic life have appealed to the philosopher's purportedly unique degree of freedom. Rousseau does not explicitly make such a claim himself, but he does perhaps do so implicitly and most indirectly. Rousseau no sooner cites freedom as a human distinction than he alludes to the "difficulties" facing any claim to free will, which might seem to call into question the significance and even the reality of human freedom. And yet the problems attaching to the claim of freedom only redound to the benefit of the philosophers' claim to freedom, for if philosophers have no more freedom of will than others, they understand why this is so. They understand the compelling character of the apparent good, i.e., that human beings always do what seems best to them to do. And this understanding bespeaks a considerable degree of a kind of freedom that incontrovertibly *is* possible for a human being, namely, freedom of *mind*.

Alas, Rousseau does not explicitly identify freedom of mind as a mark of human distinctiveness or even as the mark of the philosopher. And so the case for philosophers as natural human beings, insofar as it rests on a claim to freedom, is not airtight. Further support for the naturalness of the philosophic life, however, can be found by considering the faculty of self-perfection, the second natural human distinction—or perhaps it's the first, for, later in the *Second Discourse*, buried deep into a long note, Rousseau refers to this faculty as *the* human distinction (*SD*, 214). Here too we are faced with a certain difficulty. The faculty of self-perfection is only the name for the capacity to change; it consists only in possibility, and in an enormous range of possibilities at that. Can such an open-ended and non-teleological capacity provide the basis for establishing that one way of life is more natural than another? In fact it can, if we consider what makes that capacity so meaningful and important—namely, *the expansiveness of human self-love*, the expansiveness of human self-love *as such*, not only amour-propre but *amour de soi* as well.

Earlier we noted Rousseau's lament concerning thinking that constricts his being (or, which is the same thing, his sentiment of being) and his embrace of thinking that enlarges or expands his being. What we have not yet noted is that it belongs to our species to want or to desire more being and to seek it either in good ways or bad. Rousseau sees human beings as innately characterized by a reaching-beyond-themselves, by a desire to have or rather to *be* more. In *Emile* he speaks of "the desire to extend our being" (*E*, 168). In the *Dialogues*, employing a terminology reminiscent of modern physics, he observes at work in human beings "the positive or attracting action...of nature, which seeks to extend and reinforce the feeling of our being" (*D*, 112). He does not explicitly cite this desire and reaching-out as a human distinction, but it surely is one in his view. Arguably it is the most important human distinction of all by virtue of what it has allowed and propelled human beings to do and make, including, especially, what they have done *to* and made *of* themselves. If this expansiveness distinguishes human beings from other animals, it also distinguishes philosophers *among* human beings. Not that philosophers are by nature uniquely possessed of any desire or faculty. Rather, philosophers have attained more of what is universally wanted. The philosophic life is distinct from other lives; it is more fully realized and therefore *more natural* than other lives, because it is a life of the *most* extended being. It fulfills the natural passion or meta-passion for expanded being—in at least four ways.[29]

First, philosophic reflection can enable us to disabuse ourselves of prejudices and delusions that give rise to irrational hopes and fears and thus to the diminishment of our being. In Rousseau's own case as depicted in the *Reveries*, such reflection, in combination with intense introspection, led to the realization that he hadn't been living according to the wisdom he had long been professing, and why this was so. Although he had long professed to have resigned himself to what he could not change, he discovered that in fact he hadn't: a petty self-pride posing as a noble passion for justice had continued to stoke his outrage.

Correcting bad thinking or disabusing oneself of harmful prejudices and delusions, as important as it is, contributes to the extension of one's being only negatively and indirectly. The remaining ways in which philosophy can contribute to the extension of one's being are direct, or, rather, *immediate*.[30]

Second, philosophy can also contribute to the enlargement of one's being by exercising capacities of the soul that would otherwise be un- or underemployed. "To live is not to breathe, it is to act; it is to make use of all our organs, our senses, our faculties, of all the parts of ourselves which give us the sentiment of existence" (*E*, 42). We *are*, we experience *being*, through activity. And philosophizing is indeed activity. To be sure, Rousseau refers to various of his intellectual pursuits as *idle*. But "idle" (*oiseuse*) as he

[29] The following discussion draws on an analysis I have elaborated in prior publications. See especially "Between Eros and Will to Power," chap. 5 in *Eros*.

[30] Most Rousseau scholars, including many of the finest, hold—erroneously, in my view—that philosophy in Rousseau's view can be helpful *only* in the indirect way I've just described and not in the direct ways I'm about to state. See, for example, Christopher Kelly, *Rousseau as Author: Consecrating One's Life to the Truth* (Chicago: University of Chicago Press, 2003), 172–82.

uses the term means only that the purpose of an activity does not lie beyond enjoyment of the activity itself. This is why Rousseau can describe his botanizing as an "idle occupation" despite acknowledging in the same passage that he "examines each flower with interest and curiosity" and that this examination yields pleasure precisely when he "begins to *grasp* [*saisir*] the laws of their structure" (*R*, 98; emphasis added). Most of us, in Rousseau's view, would be well advised *not* to exercise certain faculties of mind, or not to exercise them too ambitiously, since the result is likely to be the incitement of unfulfillable desire or intense anxiety and thus the *diminishment* of our being. But what is dangerous for most is not dangerous for all, or at least not too dangerous to be worth pursuing.

Third, through philosophy one might transcend narrow egoism, whose inherent defensiveness necessarily entails constrictive fear, dread, and anxiety. This transcendence can be understood both negatively and positively—both as freeing oneself from thralldom to amour-propre or the sense that one's well-being depends on one's relative standing in the world, and as insight into the true nature of the self.

Fourth and finally, human beings have capacities and qualities which somehow correspond to various phenomena in the external world, such that contemplating those phenomena can activate or further activate the corresponding capacities and qualities. These correspondences have been recognized as critical to Rousseau's aesthetics.[31] I suggest that they are pertinent to Rousseau's conception of the philosophic life as well.

***

Thus far we have considered the case for philosophers as natural human beings on the grounds of the ordering and governance of

[31] Kelly, *Rousseau as Author*, 181.

their souls. But that case can also be made, indeed needs to be made, on the grounds that philosophers have clearer and more capacious vision, that they come closest to seeing nature as it is—that they see it naturally, as it were. Recall Rousseau's account in *Reveries* 7 of his newly improved way of looking at the world. Ostensibly he is speaking there about his botanizing, but his invocations of "the system of beings" and "the whole of nature" indicate that he is also and indeed primarily speaking of himself as philosopher. Not that the two cases for the philosopher's naturalness are truly independent of one another. Indeed, each seems to require or presuppose the other. Philosophers are able to see as clearly as they do because they are not tyrannized by amour-propre. And they elude amour-propre's despotism because they see as clearly as they do. Their freedom of mind (clear sight of what is) is made possible by their freedom of soul (freedom from amour-propre's tyranny), and vice versa. This mutual causality might seem to indicate a fatal circularity for all who aren't preternaturally gifted. In fact, though, the circularity needn't be fatal, and in the case of the philosopher it isn't. For that matter the circularity needn't always be fatal even where the rest of us are concerned, for amour-propre's despotism needn't be and perhaps never is *perfect* despotism, and our sight needn't be and perhaps never is *utterly* distorted. And so there exists the possibility of a *happy* circularity, wherein freedom of mind and freedom of soul support and enhance one another. We see this possibility actualized in the *Reveries*, in which, as I noted earlier, Rousseau tells the story of his own philosophic life in its coming-to-be, its being, and its ongoing development.

The story is too complex to be briefly summarized. However, there is one element that bears noting, for this element is perhaps the decisive mark of the philosopher. *The philosopher for Rousseau is one who has transcended what I call the ordinary moral consciousness in favor of what I call the cognitivist view of morality.* By the ordinary moral consciousness I mean the presuppositions that underpin moral judgment as we normally understand it, according to which right and wrong actions are done by individuals who know or should have known right and wrong and who may therefore be praised or blamed in accordance with the free choice they have made. The cognitivist view of morality, by contrast, holds that everyone acts in pursuit of what he or she takes to be good—that one's actions necessarily follow from, indeed are compelled by, what one takes to be good—and thus that right and wrong actions arise, respectively, from right judgment (either knowledge or right opinion) and wrong judgment (error or ignorance). Overcoming the ordinary moral consciousness in favor of the cognitivist view of morality is necessary to the philosophic life in Rousseau's view, first, because it is true—we are compelled by the apparent good—and second, because the incoherence of the ordinary moral consciousness inevitably skews our sight of much else.[32]

---

[32] The view of the philosopher as one who has transcended the ordinary moral consciousness in favor of the cognitivist view of morality is hardly original with Rousseau. It is communicated by classical political philosophers as well—not straightforwardly, but emphatically. Regarding the different ways in which arguments for the cognitivist view of morality (though not by that name) are made in five Platonic dialogues, see Lorraine Pangle, *Virtue is Knowledge: The Moral Foundations of Socratic Political Philosophy* (Chicago: The University of Chicago Press, 2014). For a detailed and exceptionally frank unpacking of how the argument is made in the *Apology of Socrates*, see David Leibowitz, *The Ironic Defense of Socrates: Plato's "Apology"* (New York: Cambridge University Press, 2010), 120–29. Aristotle too makes the case for the cognitivist view of morality, arguably more boldly than Plato, in that he considers outright the radical premises from which it follows. To be sure, he goes on to rebut these premises. But one might well deem these rebuttals weaker than that which they rebut, and knowingly so. See the *Nicomachean Ethics*, book 3, chapter 5.

If transcending the ordinary moral consciousness in favor of the cognitivist view of morality signifies that one has embarked on the philosophic life, *more perfectly* transcending the ordinary moral consciousness in favor of the cognitivist view signifies that one has *further perfected* the philosophic life. Rousseau's movement toward this further perfection is the main plotline of the *Reveries.* At the start of the book Rousseau already professes the cognitivist view, but as the action of the book shows, he hasn't yet taken it truly to heart. It is only with his further perfection as a student of nature that he is finally able to see that he hasn't been able to let go of the ordinary moral consciousness and embrace the cognitivist view. The decisive moment of his further perfection as a student of nature is recounted in the Seventh Walk, in which we see him newly able to apprehend nature as a system. This philosophic breakthrough seems to be what allows him finally to discover, in the Eighth Walk, that he has heretofore been fooled by "petty self-pride," a species of amour-propre that has been falsely passing itself off as a noble passion for justice.

Overcoming the ordinary moral consciousness does not mean overcoming morality as such or moral concern and obligation, though it might seem to from the perspective of the ordinary moral consciousness. Morality does come to be understood differently, however. "Just" and "unjust" now refer respectively to what is good or healthful to do and what is bad or unhealthful to do. What is at issue between the ordinary moral consciousness and the cognitivist view of morality is, at bottom, the question of human freedom. Those governed by the ordinary moral consciousness presume that people freely choose to do what they do and that our choices and deeds are therefore rightly subject to moral praise and blame. Yet even the fiercest defenders of the ordinary moral consciousness admit that this rule doesn't always hold: sometimes we act *un*freely, either because we have been compelled or because we have acted in ignorance, and in those instances we should not be held blameworthy. The critique of the ordinary moral consciousness begins by asking whether what the ordinary moral consciousness allows as an exception isn't in fact the rule—not because someone is coercing us or keeping important information from us, but simply because we always do, we are always *compelled* to do, whatever seems good for us to do. If we act badly, it is because we are in error regarding what would be good to do. But are we not responsible for that error? In part, yes: we think for ourselves and we habituate ourselves to certain views by acting as we do. But in deeper part, no. Yes, we think for ourselves; but we began to do so only when released from the tutelage of others. Yes, we play a great role in shaping our own judgment and character; but the self that took on this role was not self-created. This is by no means to deny human freedom, though, again, it is bound to seem so to the ordinary moral consciousness. Rather, it is to identify the true locus and nature of our freedom. Our freedom is freedom of mind. We can reflect on and change what it is that seems good to us. We can make progress toward a truer vision of the good (as, of course, we can devolve toward a more erroneous vision of the good). But this freedom, though natural, must be won. And according to Rousseau, as to the Socratics he follows in this, the winning is a rare and difficult thing.

Neither the goodness nor the naturalness of a way of life is called into question by its being beyond the reach of most or even all people, so long as it is accessible in principle, i.e., to a perfectly formed and healthy human being. Nor does the remoteness of the philosophic life render it any less meaningful to us from whom it lies beyond reach. For if we wish to understand ourselves and in any way orient our lives in relation to nature, we should look to the perfectly natural, understanding by that term not only the absence of corruption but also complete development. Which, as it happens, is exactly what Rousseau says we should do—not only in the *Reveries* and *Emile* but also, of all places, at the start of the *Second Discourse*, with the epigraph he has drawn from Aristotle's *Politics*:

> *What is natural has to be considered in*
> *what is good according to nature, not in*
> *what is corrupt.*[33]

[33] Aristotle, *Politics*, 1254a36–38. Rousseau's epigraph appeared in Latin: *Non in depravatis, sed in his quæ bene secundum naturam se habent, considerandum est quid sit naturale.* Those who regard the *Second Discourse* as Rousseau's decisive statement on nature regard his choice of epigraphs as ironic. And so it is, though not in the way these readers suppose.

3.

PRIDE PRECEDES THE RUIN OF THE SOUL: ON ROUSSEAU'S USE OF *ORGUEIL* IN THE *SECOND DISCOURSE*

Emma Planinc

The role of pride in Rousseau's political philosophy has become central to interpretive debates. Instigated especially by the studies of Nicholas Dent and Frederick Neuhouser,[1] the possibility for the positive manifestation of amour-propre (pride)[2] in Rousseau's work is a prevalent, if not dominant, reading. This reading seems to disrupt a distinction made by Rousseau in the *Discourse on the Origin and Foundations of Inequality Among Men* (hereafter *Second Discourse*), in which amour-propre (pride) is starkly divided from *amour-de-soi-même* [self-love] and condemned as a harmful artifice. There are "two passions," Rousseau writes, that "must not be confused. Self-love [*amour-de-soi-même*] is a natural feeling that inclines every animal to look after its own self-preservation and that, directed in man by reason and modified by pity,

[1] N. J. H. Dent and T. O'Hagan, "Rousseau on Amour-Propre," *Proceedings of the Aristotelian Society, Supplementary Volumes* 72 (1998): 57–75; Frederick Neuhouser, *Rousseau's Theodicy of Self-Love: Evil, Rationality, and the Drive for Recognition* (Oxford: Oxford University Press, 2008).

[2] Amour-propre is translated differently by most interpreters of Rousseau. I will follow John Scott's translation here, and will discuss the translations of pride in section 2.

produces humanity and virtue. Pride [amour-propre] is only a relative feeling, fabricated and born in society, that inclines every individual to attach more importance to himself than to anyone else, [and] that inspires in men all the harm they do to one another.... This being well understood, I say that in our primitive state, in the genuine state of nature, pride [amour-propre] does not exist" (*SD*, 147; *OC*, III.219).[3] The natural state for human beings—one of natural goodness—has no place for pride, which engenders comparisons between men and thus instigates inequality and vice.

Nicholas Dent concedes that accounts of amour-propre in Rousseau share the ruinous warnings about relationality and inequality, or the need for comparison and rank in human civilization; nevertheless, he argues that it is possible to see a positive and generative role for amour-propre in Rousseau's writings about education and politics. Seeing amour-propre as a kind of developed form of *amour-de-soi-même*, Dent maintains the separation of the two passions while interpreting Rousseau as allowing for a productive pridefulness in our unnatural circumstances.[4] Similarly, Frederick Neuhouser argues in *Rousseau's Theodicy of Self-Love* that like Augustine and Hobbes before him, Rousseau saw pride as the central issue of the human condition; "yet Rousseau's understanding of the role that amour-propre plays in human affairs goes significantly beyond the views of his predecessors: not only does he offer a more nuanced account of the many

[3] Hereafter, *SD*, cited by page number, refers to the *Second Discourse* in: Jean-Jacques Rousseau, *The Major Political Writings of Jean-Jacques Rousseau*, trans. and ed. John T. Scott (University of Chicago Press, 2012). Also provided will be the corresponding citation in Jean-Jacques Rousseau, *Œuvres Complètes*, ed. Bernard Gagnebin and Marcel Raymond, 5 vols. (Paris: Gallimard, Bibliothèque de la Pléiade, 1959–95), cited as *OC*, volume number. page number. Here *OC*, III.219.

[4] See Dent and O'Hagan, "Rousseau on Amour-Propre."

guises an inflamed drive for recognition can take and of the diverse problems it poses for human well-being, he also argues that solving these problems—finding a way for humans to flourish that does not require the divine transformation of their nature—depends not on suppressing or overcoming amour-propre but on cultivating it so that it contributes positively to the achievement of freedom, peace, virtue, happiness, and unalienated selfhood."[5] Many other interpreters follow Dent and Neuhouser in emphasizing the positive potentials of amour-propre, including Laurence Cooper, Timothy O'Hagan, Jonathan Marks, and Michael Locke McLendon.[6]

In his more recent study of the *Second Discourse*—*Rousseau's Critique of Inequality*—Neuhouser wants to track the distinction of *amour-de-soi-même* and amour-propre along the lines of the two books, or parts, of the text itself. The first part contains, for Neuhouser, the life of the creature of *amour-de-soi-même*; but "once the capacity (and tendency) to compare is awakened and the basic fact of social intercourse is introduced into the picture in Part II, it is no mere accident that creatures of self-love come to notice and to care about how their position compares to others'. Indeed, within the narrative of the *Second Discourse* the newly acquired ability to make simple comparisons is immediately

---

[5] Neuhouser, *Rousseau's Theodicy of Self-Love*, 2.

[6] Laurence D. Cooper, "Rousseau on Self-Love: What We've Learned, What We Might Have Learned," *The Review of Politics* 60, no. 4 (1998): 661–84; Jonathan Marks, "Who Lost Nature? Rousseau and Rousseauism," *Polity* 34, no. 4 (2002): 479–502, 478; Michael Locke McLendon, *The Psychology of Inequality: Rousseau's "Amour-Propre"* (Philadelphia: University of Pennsylvania Press, 2018). Also see Pauline Chazan, "Rousseau as Psycho-Social Moralist: The Distinction between Amour De Soi and Amour-Propre," *History of Philosophy Quarterly* 10, no. 4 (1993): 341–54; Avner Inbar, "The Rehabilitation of Amour-Propre," *History of Political Thought* 40, no. 3 (January 1, 2019): 458–83; Niko Kolodny, "The Explanation of Amour-Propre," *The Philosophical Review* 119, no. 2 (2010): 165–200.

followed by the 'first movement of pride [*orgueil*]'—a consciousness of one's superiority that, though at first only a pride in one's species, eventually turns into *amour propre*'s concern for one's standing as an individual."[7] He writes: "the process of Part II is to be understood as our own doing—as something we are responsible for in the sense that it is the product of our own free choices, and, as such, could have turned out differently."[8] Amour-propre is not a product of nature, and thus Neuhouser wants to see the divisions between parts 1 and 2 quite starkly: between the two amours, between nature and artifice, independence and dependence, isolation and society.

What Neuhouser glosses over quickly in his interpretation, however, is the foundation of my interest in the remainder of this chapter: Rousseau's choice to use the word *orgueil* (pride) when opening part 2 of the *Second Discourse* instead of the term he has already introduced and carefully defined in part 1: amour-propre. As Neuhouser notes, the "first movement of pride" that man directs upon himself opens the second part of the *Second Discourse* to the inevitable descent into inequality and vice—and this first movement is *orgueil*. Dent and Neuhouser want to see *orgueil* as a kind of transitional form of amour-propre; Dent calls *orgueil* "self-estimating *amour-de-soi*,"[9] and Neuhouser collapses *orgueil* into a kind of nascent stage of amour-propre.[10] I will argue, however, that Rousseau uses *orgueil* to begin the second part of the *Second Discourse* precisely because it has no relation to either *amour-de-soi-même* or to amour-propre. The movement of *orgueil*

[7] Frederick Neuhouser, *Rousseau's Critique of Inequality: Reconstructing the Second Discourse* (Cambridge; New York: Cambridge University Press, 2014), 75.

[8] Neuhouser, *Rousseau's Critique of Inequality*, 51.

[9] Quoted in Neuhouser, *Rousseau's Theodicy of Self-Love*, 54.

[10] Neuhouser, *Rousseau's Theodicy of Self-Love*, 46.

that man directs against himself in the second part of Rousseau's *Discourse* signals a new beginning in our understanding of human beings—a beginning that is now revisiting all of what preceded in the first part of the *Second Discourse* through the dynamic of *orgueil*, a form of pride that sees man with a pride of place, and in distinction from the natural world. The second part of the *Second Discourse* is a "new enlightenment" of man—one whose "first movement" results in a distinctive "first glance" upon ourselves that instigates all the rest of our corruptions to follow (*SD*, 92; *OC*, III.165–66). In its most radical form, my argument is that part 1 and part 2 of the *Second Discourse* are essentially the same story, written twice: first, with the movement of nature as its first premise, and second with the first movement of pride: *orgueil*.

Orgueil and amour-propre

It is necessary first to complicate the interpretation that collapses *orgueil* into amour-propre. Neuhouser's reading of the *Second Discourse* relies on a substantial separation of the first from the second part, with *amour-de-soi-même* being the hero of the first, and amour-propre the focus of the second. Neuhouser sees the *Second Discourse* as a theodicy, in which "the most innovative aspect of Rousseau's view is his claim that, despite its many dangers, amour-propre is also the condition of nearly everything that makes human existence valuable and of all that elevates it above the beasts: it is 'to this ardor to be talked about, to this furor to distinguish oneself… [that] we owe what is best and worst among men: our virtues and vices, our sciences and our errors, our conquerors and our philosophers.'"[11] Indeed, Neuhouser claims, "Rousseau goes so far as to claim that rationality, morality, and freedom—subjectivity itself—would be impossible for humans if

[11] Neuhouser, 2.

it were not for amour-propre and the relations to other subjects that it impels those who possess it to establish."[12] Though amour-propre is part of our fallen condition, for Neuhouser, because our fallenness is and was inevitable, Rousseau sees possibilities for its positive reconstitution.

According to Neuhouser, it is the "absence of *amour-propre* that makes the 'original state of nature' depicted in Part I of the *Second Discourse*... appear as such a distant and alien condition,"[13] and he even goes so far as to argue that amour-propre is "the form of self-love [that] Rousseau introduces only in Part II"[14]—a claim which is textually inaccurate, as I will discuss shortly. Neuhouser's goal is to detach amour-propre as sharply as possible from the claims of nature made in part 1 in order to argue that Rousseau constructed part 2 in opposition to it. Part 2 is to be seen as the unfolding of processes for which human beings can be held responsible. With the content of part 2 subject to human choice, that means, for Neuhouser, that its effects are reversible, but only through the appropriation of the same artificial passions and means that define the conditions of our social inequality. The distinction of part 2 is forecasted immediately for Neuhouser in the "capacity (and tendency) to compare." When this is "awakened and the basic fact of social intercourse is introduced into the picture in Part Two, it is no mere accident that creatures of self-love come to notice and to care about how their positions compare to others'. Indeed, within the narrative of the *Second Discourse* the newly acquired ability to make simple comparisons is immediately followed by the 'first movement of pride' (*orgueil*)—a consciousness of one's superiority that, though at first only a

[12] Neuhouser, 2.
[13] Neuhouser, 1.
[14] Neuhouser, 43.

pride in one's species, eventually turns into *amour-propre*'s concern for one's standing as an individual."[15]

For Neuhouser, as for Dent and other theorists of Rousseauian pride, *orgueil* is a kind of transitional passion, allowing *amour-de-soi-même* to pass over into amour-propre. Neuhouser accommodates Rousseau's strange choice to use *orgueil* when describing the first movement of pride through an interpretive disambiguation between movements directed against the species as opposed to the individual:

> because superiority over other species is advantageous for survival, even consciously intended increases in that superiority can be understood as motivated by (non-relative) *amour-de-soi-même*. Something new enters this story, however, when humans' experience of their superiority—including, interestingly, their experience of *mastery* over the less advantaged—brings with it a feeling of pleasure in occupying the higher rank, a pleasure here identified as 'the first movement of pride.'...This new and unanticipated pleasure then awakens in them a taste for superiority, perhaps even whets their appetite for more of the same, but it does not yet (as far as can be told from the text) furnish them with a positive incentive intentionally to produce conditions of superiority for the sake of enjoying even more of that pleasure. Even though it is here still only the superiority of the species that humans have learned to delight in, it is not difficult to imagine how this could be transformed into a taste for individual superiority in more complex circumstances, once differences among individuals are noticed, multiplied, and then consciously cultivated.[16]

---

[15] Neuhouser, 75.

[16] Neuhouser, 85–86.

Orgueil is thus here presented as a nascent form of amour-propre, closer to nature than civilization in its orientation to the species-level of self-identification, and not yet carrying the full consequences of developed pride.

The tripartite progression of the passions proposed here (from *amour-de-soi-même* to *orgueil* to amour-propre) does not, however, work with the structure of Rousseau's text. Despite Neuhouser's insistence that amour-propre only appears on the scene in part 2, it is not only the case that the essential note defining *amour-de-soi-même* and amour-propre is contained within part 1, but Rousseau also uses the term amour-propre *in-text* in part 1: "it is reason that engenders amour-propre, and it is reflection that fortifies it. It is reason that turns man back on himself. It is reason that separates him from everything that bothers and afflicts him" (*SD*, 84; *OC*, III.156). Following this, Rousseau uses the example of separating physical from moral love, calling the moral aspect of love an "artificial feeling born of social custom… based on certain notions of merit or beauty" (*SD*, 86; *OC*, III.158)—a love rooted in amour-propre instead of the physical *amour-de-soi-même*.

However one might want to construct the relationship between the first and second parts of Rousseau's *Second Discourse*, it is not the case that amour-propre is introduced only in part 2. Even if one were to suggest that the second part is in some sense employing the distinctions (between *amour-de-soi-même* and amour-propre) that were made in part 1, but this time in a more genealogical narrative, we would have to concede that the second part is a kind of re-starting of the first, or a new beginning. In all cases, Rousseau's decision to use *orgueil* in lieu of simply employing the term—amour-propre—that he has already conditioned the reader to accept as a kind of pridefulness in the first part of the *Discourse* is strange and deserves more interpretive nuance than it has received.

I argue in what follows that there are reasons to think that *pride* (*orgueil*) is not at all the same thing as amour-propre, or a nascent amour-propre, nor is it a slightly developed *amour-de-soi-même*. I will suggest that the second part of the *Second Discourse* is the distinctive development of amour-propre as a consequence of seeing human beings *as prideful*. That is, pride (*orgueil*) precedes amour-propre in this second part of the narrative not necessarily or genealogically in relation to the text as a whole, but because it is its own beginning, a retelling of the genesis story of part 1 from the perspective of—or given the assumption of—pride (*orgueil*). The second part of the *Second Discourse* has its own distinctive first movement, and the consequences that follow from it are also distinct, and distinctly corrupting, when human beings set themselves outside of nature in their own self-understanding and see themselves as having a pride of place.

Forms of pride

Rousseau's choice to use *orgueil* at this point in the text is intriguing not only because of its placement in the narrative, but also because of the options that were available to use in the French language when describing the first movement of pride, including amour-propre and *fierté*. Amour-propre was a term that did not appear in *La Dictionnaire de l'Académie française* until 1798—no doubt due in large part to the popularity of Rousseau's use of the term, although Rousseau was not the first to use it (amour-propre is discussed in the same way by, for example, Blaise Pascal, Pierre Nicole, and Jacques Abbadie). In the *Dictionnaire*, amour-propre is described

> in the absolute and philosophical sense, [as] the sentiment of love and the preference that each has for

> himself, and which is natural to all men: but in the most ordinary sense, it takes this same self-feeling to excess which makes it a vice; and it signifies the overly favorable opinion that man has of himself, and the overly great attachment to all that is personal to him. *This man has a lot of amour-propre. He is full of [puffed up with] amour-propre. There is a lot of amour-propre in this claim, in this language, in this response. Amour-propre is the motive of all of his actions.*"[17]

What the *Dictionnaire*'s discussion makes apparent is the overwhelmingly negative tone of the invocation of amour-propre in its common use. The difficulty of translating amour-propre has resulted in translators of Rousseau employing a wide variety of terms, many of which take on this negative connotation. Neuhouser lists them: Roger Masters calls amour-propre 'vanity,' Maurice Cranston 'pride,' and Donald Cress 'egotism,' while Allan Bloom and Victor Gourevitch both choose to leave it untranslated.[18] Neuhouser himself uses amour-propre in his work, while in his recent translations John Scott has used the term "pride."

Depending on the translation, of course, different aspects of amour-propre's definition can be invoked. Much of the recent interpretation that attempts to rescue the positive aspects of amour-propre is dependent on the ambiguity of amour-propre (even in the *Dictionnaire* there is the first more 'philosophical' definition provided), and this ambiguity is often erased with the choice of word in translation. Issues of translation and word choice aside, however, it remains the case that Rousseau himself chose to open part 2 of the *Second Discourse* not with this playful,

---

[17] "Amour propre," *La Dictionnaire de l'Académie française, Cinquième Édition* (Smits: Paris, 1798), accessed via The ARTFL Project, University of Chicago. Translation mine.

[18] Neuhouser, *Rousseau's Theodicy of Self-Love*, 54n1.

and perhaps positive, word, but with *orgueil*—a word that with no ambiguity means pride, and invokes the biblical connotation of sin.

As I have already discussed above, one interpretive "solution" to this odd choice of Rousseau's is to claim that this "first movement of pride [*orgueil*]" is a kind of transitional phase between *amour-de-soi-même*, a natural form of self-love, and amour-propre, our inflamed and comparative sense of self. This transitional phase is meant to be somewhere between nature and civilization—not belonging quite to either, but nevertheless suggesting that the possibility of a pride that is not wholly destructive remains in Rousseau's vision. If this is what is meant by Rousseau's use of a word distinct from amour-propre, however, there is a much more suitable word that he ought to have employed: *fierté*.

Fierté also means pride. All definitions of *fierté* in *La Dictionnaire de l'Académie française* connect it—unlike amour-propre or *orgueil*—to a natural or noble sense of self. The definition of *fierté* in the 1694 *Dictionnaire* describes it as the "quality of someone who is arrogant and haughty, *He is a man full of pride. He has too much pride. He has a natural pride which does him harm.... He has a noble pride.* He thinks of himself as having ferocity, cruelty, barbarous pride. *Tame lions lose their natural pride.*"[19] A very similar definition appears in the 1762 *Dictionnaire*: the "character of one who is proud. *He is a proud man. He has too much pride. He has a natural pride that does him wrong.... He has a noble pride.*"[20]

---

[19] "Fierté," *La Dictionnaire de l'Académie française* (Coignard: Paris, 1694), accessed via The ARTFL Project, University of Chicago. Translation mine.

[20] "Fierté," *La Dictionnaire de l'Académie française, Quatrième Édition* (Brunet: Paris, 1762), accessed via The ARTFL Project, University of Chicago. Translation mine.

When introducing the "first movement of pride" in part 2 of the *Second Discourse*, however, Rousseau uses neither the term he has already introduced in the first part, amour-propre, nor its natural counterpart, *fierté*. Instead he uses *orgueil*. *Orgueil* is the word for pride that carries a biblical origin. In the definitions of the *Dictionnaire* (1694, 1762) it is always connected to sinfulness and to the vanity that humans possess as sinful beings. It is also the word employed in central passages from the de Sacy (Port-Royal) Bible and is tied in the 1606 *Dictionnaire* to the Latin *superbia*, which is the word used for pride throughout the Vulgate translations of both the Hebrew and Christian scriptures.

In 1694, *orgueil* is described as "vanity, presumption, overly advantageous opinion of oneself by which one prefers oneself to others. *Strange pride, unbearable pride. Pride is the first of all the sins. Pride threw the Angels into hell....He is bursting with pride. Pride is one of the seven deadly sins.*"[21] The same definition appears in 1762: "vanity, presumption, overly advantageous opinion of oneself. *Strange pride. Unbearable pride. Pride threw the angels into hell. Do we ever live a pride the same as his? To be swollen, bloated, full of pride. I will humble, I will bring down his pride. He is bursting with pride. Pride is one of the seven deadly sins.*"[22] The first appearance of pride (*orgueil*) in the de Sacy Bible is in Leviticus, and it is used often throughout the Bible following—in Deuteronomy, Psalms and Proverbs, and Job. The appearance of "pride" only beginning in Leviticus in the de Sacy Bible is consistent with the Latin, in which *superbia* similarly does not appear in Genesis, nor

[21] "Orgueil," *La Dictionnaire de l'Académie française* (Coignard: Paris, 1694), accessed via The ARTFL Project, University of Chicago. Translation mine.

[22] "Orgueil," *La Dictionnaire de l'Académie française, Quatrième Édition* (Brunet: Paris, 1762), accessed via The ARTFL Project, University of Chicago. Translation mine.

in Exodus, but is used generously throughout the Vulgate translation to describe the pridefulness of fallen human beings.[23]

Rousseau's choice to use *orgueil* when describing the "first movement" of what will cause the fall of human beings from the state of nature is thus—to say the least—provocative. It is especially so given that Rousseau is infamous for his rejection of the doctrine of original sin, suggesting in the *Second Discourse* (and in a more developed form in the *Letter to Beaumont*) that "man is naturally good" (*SD*, 127; *OC*, III.202). It is not man's nature, but our socialization and civilization, that carries the blame for our corruption; it is not in our nature to be corrupt, but we have instead become corrupted. This principle of natural goodness, which Rousseau claimed was the foundation of his philosophy, grounds his image of natural man, who lives in a condition of *amour-de-soi-même* and demonstrates to us that "man has hardly any other evils than those he has given himself" (*SD*, 127; *OC*, III.202).

My claim is that, for Rousseau, pride (*orgueil*) is one of the evils we have given ourselves. While *amour-de-soi-même* is natural, and I think it is possible, too, to say that there is something about amour-propre that is "natural" to human beings (that it is part of our nature, perhaps, to estimate ourselves against others when properly directed), there is nothing natural about *orgueil*. *Orgueil* is an estimation of ourselves that is self-imposed; it is the presumption that we as a species are something *other than nature*, beyond nature, different from the rest—and we are so different because we estimate ourselves higher or superior. *Orgueil* is the self-imposed evil for Rousseau, and it is the perspectival shift that inaugurates the second part of the *Second Discourse*. No longer seeing ourselves through the eyes of nature, but through the eyes

---

[23] Many thanks to my colleagues Katie Bugyis and Andrew Radde-Gallwitz for their consultation on these issues of biblical translation.

of *orgueil*, we see what becomes of humanity when the first movement of our self-awareness is one of superiority and distinction. *Orgueil* is the precipitating cause of humanity's inevitable corruption in part 2—a way of self-knowing or self-seeing that is inherently pleonectic, and which we would be better off without. If we see the dangers of the evils we have caused ourselves, Rousseau writes in his note on natural goodness, we would "deplore man's blindness, which, to feed his foolish pride [*orgueil*] and I know not what vain admiration for himself, makes him rush ardently after all the miseries to which he is susceptible and which beneficent nature had taken care to keep from him" (*SD*, 127; *OC*, III.202).

In *Rousseau's God*, John Scott marks the connection between the use of *orgueil* in Rousseau's work and the invocation of God, or divine providence: "the human desire to be worthy, even the worthiest, in the eyes of divinity is owing to pride."[24] In his analysis of Rousseau's *Letter to Voltaire*, Scott writes: "up to this point, it was a question of knowing how things, including human things, appear 'in the eyes of nature,' but now we have the demand of the individual for recognition from on high: 'I believe, I hope, I am worth more *in the eyes of God* than the land of a planet.' What, then, of the probable inhabitants of Saturn or other planets? The individual still hopes to be worth more. In the end, Rousseau admits that 'it is only human pride [*orgueil*]' that underlies this belief or hope."[25] When we imagine how things appear "'in the eyes of God,' pride [*orgueil*] enters the stage, and the scene changes."[26] It is my suggestion that it is precisely such a scene change that we experience in part 2 of the *Second Discourse*;

[24] John T. Scott, *Rousseau's God: Theology, Religion, and the Natural Goodness of Man* (Chicago: The University of Chicago Press, 2023), 102.

[25] Scott, 114–15. Emphasis added.

[26] Scott, 101–2.

a re-beginning of the natural story of part 1 through the eyes of prideful, and sinfully self-estimating, human beings.

Through the eyes of pride

Part 2 of the *Second Discourse* is the distinctive development of human beings as a consequence of seeing ourselves as prideful. Pride precedes amour-propre in this second narrative not necessarily or genealogically in relation to the text as a whole, but because it is its own beginning, a retelling of the genesis story of part 1. Part 2 is part 1 with the addition of *orgueil*. Put another way, part 2 is a re-founding, or a re-seeing, of the story of human nature from the perspective of—or given the assumption of—pride (*orgueil*, not amour-propre).

First, to the reasons why I believe *orgueil* occupies its own space, pointing us toward thinking of it as a unique addition to Rousseau's story of the human being—and perhaps, if I am persuasive, also pointing toward *orgueil* equaling the importance of amour-propre in this text (the former is mentioned six times, and the latter seven). On multiple occasions in the first part of the *Second Discourse*, Rousseau claims that amour-propre is tied to reason. In part 2, when we see the first movement of pride, it is very specifically *not* tied to reason, but instead to what Rousseau calls a "mechanical prudence"—a capacity that humans and animals share, which tends to their own self-preservation. The "naturally" engendered relations that are perceived by the man who experiences the first movements of *orgueil* are not the same as the relations that we might experience through amour-propre. Amour-propre is also always tied to intersubjective comparison, whereas in the case of *orgueil*, the comparison that is enacted is to other animals—with man understanding himself *as human* (as being of a kind, of the species, human) as opposed to in relation to (or refracted through) other humans themselves.

Amour-propre only comes into play once one is comparing oneself to other persons—understanding oneself as an 'I' in relation to others. In *Emile*, Rousseau describes the transition from *amour-de-soi-même* to amour-propre on precisely these grounds: "the first glance [Emile] casts on his fellows leads him to compare himself with them. And the first sentiment aroused in him by this comparison is the desire to be in the first position. This is the point where love of self turns into *amour-propre* and where begin to arise all the passions which depend on this one" (*E*, 235; *OC*, IV.523).[27]

Orgueil, then, seems to occupy a kind of middling place. It is naturally comparative, not artificially, and it is not individually relational, but a relation only of the species to other species (or an awareness of oneself as human that is not an awareness of oneself *as an individual*). As I have already discussed, all interpreters who accommodate *orgueil* into a reading of pride in Rousseau's work see it transitionally: as a step away from part 1 into part 2, insofar as we are on the way to amour-propre, and away from part 1. But I don't think this is right. This is because everything that surrounds *orgueil* is *already present* in part 1 (including, as I discuss above, amour-propre), and in some cases described almost identically with only one omission—the omission of *orgueil* itself.

The "first movement of pride" at the beginning of Part 2 appears as follows:

> The repeated utilizations of various beings in relation to himself and of some beings in relation to others must naturally have engendered perceptions of certain relations in man's mind. Those relations that we express by the words "large, "small," "strong," "weak," "fast,"

[27] *E*, cited by page number, will refer to Rousseau's *Emile: Or On Education*, trans. Allan Bloom (New York: Basic Books, 1979).

"slow," "fearful," "bold," and other similar ideas, compared when necessary, and almost without thinking about it, eventually produced in him reflection of a sort, or rather a mechanical prudence that indicated to him the precautions most necessary for his safety.

The new enlightenment that resulted from this development increased his superiority over the other animals by making him aware of it. He practiced setting traps for them, he tricked them in a thousand ways, and although some of them surpassed him in strength in combat or speed in running, in time he became the master of those that might serve him and the scourge of those that might harm him. This is how the first glance he directed upon himself produced in him the first movement of pride [*orgueil*]. This is how, as yet scarcely knowing how to distinguish ranks and looking upon himself as in the first rank as a species, he prepared himself from afar to claim the first rank as an individual. (*SD*, 92; *OC*, III.165–66)

In part 1, however, Rousseau describes physical, natural man as follows:

Savage man, living dispersed among the animals and early finding himself in the position of having to measure himself against them, soon makes the comparison, and, sensing that he surpasses them in skill more than they surpass him in strength, he learns to fear them no more....With regard to those animals that actually have more strength than man has skill, he is in the same position with respect to them as other weaker species, which nonetheless continue to subsist, with this advantage for man: that, no less prepared than they are to run and finding almost certain refuge in trees, he always has the offer of accepting or refusing the encounter and the choice of fleeing or fighting. (*SD*, 67; *OC*, III.136)

This is, by all accounts, the same description of man. There is a species-awareness, a comparative prudence, and an awareness too, of a kind, that there is a freedom of choice in one's actions. What is lacking in this mirrored passage in part 1 are all the things that we associate with pride—and in particular, pride of the sort we would call *orgueil.* The distinctive thing that is missing in the description in the first part, but is contained in part 2, is the language of mastery, of dominion over the other species, of the fateful self-direction of a human being recognizing himself as superior—paving the way, as it proceeds in part 2, for the affirmation of individual superiority against others.

The whole sequence of the argument in part 1, I contend, offers everything you can also get from part 2. We have in part 1 the distinction of the physical from the metaphysical, and the distinction of *amour-de-soi-même* from amour-propre; of "an animal less strong than some, less agile than others" from one possessed of enlightenment and "supernatural gifts" (*SD*, 66; *OC*, III.134–35). This mirrors the development of amour-propre out of our presumably natural state in part 2—from man's first feeling of his existence and first care of his preservation (*SD*, 91; *OC*, III.164) to the emergence of amour-propre, when "the goodness suitable to the pure state of nature" (*SD*, 96–97; *OC*, III.170) was no longer present. For, as Rousseau writes in the second part, "from the moment that one man needed the help of another, as soon as they perceived it was useful for a single person to have provisions for two, equality disappeared, property was introduced, labor became necessary, and vast forests were changed into smiling fields which had to be watered by the sweat of men and in which slavery and misery were soon seen to sprout and grow together with the harvest" (*SD*, 97; *OC*, III.171).

The possessive, property-driven narrative of the second part begins immediately with Rousseau's opening sentence: "the first person who, having enclosed a plot of ground, thought of saying *this is mine* and found people simple enough to believe him, was the true founder of civil society" (*SD*, 91; *OC*, III.164). While Rousseau is certainly engaging with John Locke in the *Second Discourse*, it is the case that the texture, or scene, of the narrative changes so dramatically in the Second Part because the emphasis on possession and ownership—on *mine* and *thine*—is grounded in a conception of *dominion*. The foundation of John Locke's *Second Treatise*, which he shares with the biblical narrative, is that God gave the earth to all the creatures in common, thus establishing a kind of equality. Human beings, however, have a pride of place in this gift—a special sort of means of enacting their dominion through possessing land and, ultimately, possessing and exerting mastery over persons.

It is *orgueil* that grants (or purports to grant) this dominion—over the earth, the animals, and each other. When man experiences the "first movement" of *orgueil* it is a feeling of superiority and of placing himself as first in rank *as a species*; that is, by virtue of being human and nothing else. *Orgueil* is an a priori presumption of superiority, not generatively relative like amour-propre, properly considered. Once amour-propre is reintroduced in the narrative of the Second Part of the *Second Discourse*, it is already doomed to emerge in its corrupted form engendering destructive inequalities, because its first movement is now one of *orgueil* instead of one of nature or *amour-de-soi-même*.

I am here suggesting a perspectival reading of the *Second Discourse*, with two perspectives of the creation provided in two movements: of what man was and how we have come to be. The first part is a creation story of man as he would be considered as a human species, in and with the natural order; the second part is a creation story of man considered as a human species when and because he considers himself to be superior, having a *pride of place*. The substance of the story is the same *until the addition of orgueil*, which is not a distinction of material but of perception—a superimposition of how we perceive ourselves that colors the rest of the narrative. It is *orgueil*—pride, dominion, mastery, and all of the property claims that come along with it—that makes man what he is now, as we see him, and this is our narrative precisely because we apply it to, or perceive it in, ourselves.

In his *Letter to Beaumont*, Rousseau makes more explicit his claim that man is born good and with a natural love of self (*amour-de-soi-même*):

> the fundamental principle of all morality about which I have reasoned in all of my writings and developed in this last one with all the clarity of which I was capable is that man is a naturally good being, loving justice and order; that there is no original perversity in the human heart, and *that the first movements of nature are always right*. I have shown that the only passion born with man, namely love of self, is a passion that is in itself indifferent to good and evil; that it becomes good or bad only by accident and depending on the circumstances in which it develops. I have shown that all the vices imputed to the human heart are not natural to it; I have stated the manner in which they are born. I have followed their genealogy, so to speak, and have shown how, through continuous deterioration of their original

goodness, men finally become what they are. (*LB*, 28; *OC*, IV.935–36).[28]

Beaumont's objection to Rousseau's system, he says, is "to oppose me with original sin" (*LB*, 29; *OC*, IV.937). "The cause of evil," Rousseau continues, "according to you, is corrupted nature, and this corruption itself is an evil whose cause has to be sought. Man was created good. We both agree on that, I believe. But you say he is wicked because he was wicked. And I show how he was wicked. Which of us, in your opinion, better ascends to the principle?" (*LB*, 31; *OC*, IV.940). It is thus Rousseau's contention in the *Letter to Beaumont* that he explains the principle of original sin better than the theologians. While certainly this is written with some cheek, and is no doubt intentionally inflammatory, I take Rousseau at his word. His goal, he continues in the *Letter* is not to curb vice, but to "prevent it from being born" (*LB*, 33; *OC*, IV.942): "if man is good by his nature, as I believe I have demonstrated, it follows that he remains so as long as nothing foreign to himself spoils him. And if men are wicked, as they have gone to the trouble of teaching me, it follows that their wickedness comes from elsewhere. Close the entrance to vice, then, and the human heart will always be good" (*LB*, 35; *OC*, IV.945).

In the *Second Discourse*, Rousseau has provided a window to the entrance to vice, the source of wickedness, and the cause of our corruption. It is not that we are creatures of original sin; rather, the issue is that we have supplanted our natural self-conception with a perception of ourselves as sinful. *The first movement of nature*, which is always right, is in part 2 replaced with, or

---

[28]*LB*, cited by page number, refers to Jean-Jacques Rousseau, "Letter to Beaumont," in *The Collected Writings of Rousseau*, vol. 9 (Hanover, NH: University Press of New England, 1990). Emphasis mine.

supplanted by, *the first movement of orgueil. Orgueil* is itself, for Rousseau, the source of human dominion and domination, the modifying factor, the poison at the root of our self-conception. We can see this in the *Second Discourse* precisely because we have been provided an alternative: we get a narrative with this destructive human pridefulness (part 2), and a narrative without (part 1). The ingredient, or circumstance, that inalterably changes the course of events, and the way that we think of ourselves, is given to us by Rousseau in plain sight: it is our own estimation of ourselves as sinful and prideful creatures from the beginning—*as a second beginning, or a distinct first movement.* If we can close or eradicate the perception of ourselves as pridefully superior, then we may, it seems, open ourselves back up to the first movement that is *right*—the first movement of nature and the good.

Orgueil is the foreign element about which Rousseau speaks in the *Letter to Beaumont*, and the beginning of the story of our fall. As long as the first movement of our self-understanding is one of *orgueil*, the human soul is doomed to corruption. This is a self-perception that is antithetical to our nature, which is good, and so its wickedness is alien and spoils the soul. Rousseau, I believe, thinks that he has explicated perfectly the operation of original sin and the fall of man. As Proverbs 16:18 states in the Bible de Sacy: "*L'orgueil précède la ruine de l'âme, et l'esprit s'élève avent la chute*" ("pride precedes the ruin of the soul, and a haughty [elevated] spirit before a fall"). This ruin of the soul, for those of us who are prideful and who believe in the human pride of place, is indeed self-inflicted for as long as we perceive ourselves to be creatures of original sin. What is illuminated for us by Rousseau in the *Second Discourse* is his alternative account of what man could have been by nature—what we are still, perhaps, if and once we perceive a different beginning, or an alternative first movement to that of *orgueil.*

4.

THE PROBLEM OF KNOWLEDGE IN ROUSSEAU'S *SECOND DISCOURSE*

Samuel A. Stoner

Common readers, pardon me my paradoxes. When one reflects, they are necessary and whatever you may say, I prefer to be a paradoxical man than a prejudiced one.[1]

Descartes has been honored as the father of modern philosophy, and he is one of the great early theorists and defenders of methodical, mathematical physics and the useful technologies it promises.[2] Rousseau is among the first great critics of modern philosophy, and his critique of modernity emerges as an account of the forms of degradation effected by the advance of the sciences and the arts.[3] Even as he decries the influence of efforts like Descartes's to institute the new science and its practical fruits as organizing principles of human life, however, Rousseau praises Descartes as a "vast genius" destined to join those "preceptors of

[1] Jean-Jacques Rousseau, *Emile, or On Education*, trans. Allan Bloom (New York: Basic Books, 1979), 93.

[2] See Part Six of René Descartes, *Discourse on Method*, trans. Richard Kennington (Newburyport: Focus Publishing, 2007). Cf. Richard Kennington's essays on Descartes in *On Modern Origins: Essays in Early Modern Philosophy*, eds. Pamela Kraus and Frank Hunt (Lanham: Lexington Books, 2004).

[3] See Rousseau's *Discourse on the Sciences and the Arts* in Jean-Jacques Rousseau, *The Major Political Writings of Jean-Jacques Rousseau*, trans. John T. Scott (Chicago: University of Chicago Press, 2012).

the human race" who "raise monuments to the glory of the human mind" (*FD*, 34–35).[4] Rousseau is both a critic and an admirer of Descartes.

Thinking through Rousseau's approach to Descartes carries us toward the heart of his philosophical project, illuminating the premises of his critique of modernity, highlighting the modernity of these premises, and clarifying the intentions that govern his writing. This essay will argue that Rousseau enacts a radical confrontation with Descartes in the *Discourse on the Origin and the Foundations of Inequality Among Men*. Attending to the problem of knowledge in the *Second Discourse* reveals that Rousseau is and is not a Cartesian.

Knowledge in Rousseau's *Second Discourse*

Rousseau emphasizes the problem of knowledge in the *Second Discourse* from the opening sentence of the Preface: "the most useful and the least advanced of all human knowledge appears to me to be that of man, and I dare say that the inscription on the Temple of Delphi alone contained a more important and more difficult precept than all the hefty books of the moralists" (*SD*, 51).[5] Knowledge of human nature is useful because it promises to disclose the principles that ought to govern human life. But, attaining such knowledge is difficult—not only because "all the

---

[4]Hereafter, *FD* refers to the *First Discourse*, or *Discourse on the Sciences and the Arts*, in *The Major Political Writings of Jean-Jacques Rousseau*, cited by page. Rousseau names three modern natural philosophers who fall into this exclusive class: Bacon, Descartes, and Newton. Is it an accident of history that Descartes is the central figure?

[5]*SD* will be used to refer to the *Second Discourse*, or *Discourse on the Origin and Foundations of Inequality among Men*, in *The Major Political Writings of Jean-Jacques Rousseau*. For a helpful account of the problem of self-knowledge in Rousseau's major writings, see Benjamin Storey, "Rousseau and the Problem of Self-Knowledge," *Review of Politics* 71 (2009): 251–74.

changes that the succession of times and of things" have wrought in human beings obscure human nature, but also because the advancement of learning has carried humanity ever further from its original condition, making the essential nature of the human increasingly difficult to discern (*SD*, 51). The search for knowledge threatens to undermine the possibility of the most important form of knowledge.

If Rousseau begins the *Second Discourse* by highlighting the problem of self-knowledge, however, he proceeds to address it. The *Second Discourse* itself is a meditation—Rousseau uses this Cartesian word repeatedly and conscientiously—on the nature of the human being that seeks to uncover the hitherto concealed essence of the human:

> Setting aside...all scientific books that teach us only to see men as they have made themselves, and meditating on the first and simplest operations of the human soul, I believe I perceive in it two principles preceding reason, one of which interests us ardently in our well-being and our self-preservation, and the other of which inspires in us a natural repugnance to seeing any sensitive being, and principally our fellow humans, perish or suffer. (*SD*, 54)

Rousseau claims that his quest for knowledge of human nature reveals two basic psychological principles that precede reason, illuminate its origin, explain its genesis, condition its quest for knowledge, and so serve as starting points for his account of the genesis of human thinking and knowing.

Once they emerge, reason and knowledge play an integral role in human history. Immediately after introducing perfectibility as the capacity that, "with the aid of circumstances, successively develops all the others" (*SD*, 72), Rousseau describes the dynamic that underlies and explains the development of human psychology and, a fortiori, human history:

> Whatever the moralists may say about it, human understanding owes much to the passions which, as is generally acknowledged, owe much to it as well. It is by their activity that our reason is perfected. We seek to know only because we desire to have pleasure, and it is not possible to conceive why someone who had neither desires nor fears would go to the trouble of reasoning. The passions, in turn, derive their origin from our needs and their progress from our knowledge. (*SD*, 73)

Our needs generate passions, these passions cause reason to seek knowledge, the knowledge reason attains enhances our powers, our awareness of our strengthened powers generates new passions, these new passions drive us to seek new knowledge, and so on. Circumstances and the passions they provoke are the proximate material and efficient causes of humanity's development, but reason and the knowledge it discovers are the formal clauses that determine the direction and progression of human history.

The latter insight runs like a guiding thread through part 2 of the *Second Discourse* and culminates in Rousseau's claim in this work's final paragraph that the account of human history it presents entails "that inequality, being almost nonexistent in the state of nature, derives its force and growth from the development of our faculties *and from the progress of the human mind*" (*SD*, 117, emphasis mine).[6] It is not simply the advent of amour-propre and the tyrannical passions that follow in its wake, but also

[6] Cf. Rousseau's characterization of the task of part 2 of the *Second Discourse* at the end of part 1: "after having proved that inequality is barely perceptible in the state of nature and that its influence there is almost nonexistent, it remains for me to show its origin and its progress *in the successive developments of the human mind*" (*SD*, 89, emphasis mine).

the development of the mind's capacity to reflect, reason, and know that generates moral inequality and the forms of misery characteristic of social existence. The genesis of reason and knowledge is at least half the history.

The Still Soul of Natural Man

Rousseau begins his pursuit of knowledge of the nature of the human in part 1 of the *Second Discourse* by "stripping" the human being "of all the supernatural gifts he could have received and of all the artificial faculties he could have acquired only by prolonged progress" (*SD*, 66). Rousseau adopts a skeptical posture, denying humanity all characteristics and capacities he possibly can while preserving a being that is recognizably human—i.e., a being who has all and only the characteristics and capacities that are necessary to account for humanity's development into its current condition. In this way, Rousseau proposes to uncover the original, unadulterated being of the human "such as he must have come from the hands of nature" (*SD*, 66).

Rousseau's procedure, here, anticipates Kant's transcendental approach to philosophical problems, which begins with the fact of human experience and proceeds regressively, uncovering the principles that constitute the necessary conditions of a particular form of human experience in order to demonstrate the legitimacy of these principles and of the form of experience they ground.[7] But, the closer analogue and the inspiration for Rousseau's way of thinking in the *Second Discourse* is Descartes's *Meditations on First Philosophy*. In the First Meditation, we learn that the meditator's strong desire to "establish" something "firm and

[7] For a helpful account of Kant's transcendental approach to philosophical problems and an overview of Kant's application of this approach in his critical philosophy, see Karl Ameriks, *Interpreting Kant's* Critiques (Oxford: Oxford University Press, 2003), 1–48.

lasting in the sciences" leads him to doubt every opinion he can possibly doubt in hopes of discovering an indubitable truth that can serve as the unshakeable foundation for scientific knowledge.[8] Subsequently, in the Second Meditation, the meditator's reflections on a melting piece of wax reveal that the mind can only attain knowledge of the essence of a being by "stripping it" of "its external forms."[9]

Rousseau, too, claims that his intense desire for knowledge drives him to seek a firm foundation for the knowledge he seeks. This point is indicated by the full title of the *Second Discourse*—

[8] René Descartes, *Meditations, Objections, and Replies*, ed. and trans. Roger Ariew and Donald Cress (Indianapolis: Hackett, 2006), 9. On the significance of the genre of meditation and the distinction between Descartes, the author of the *Meditations*, and the meditator he depicts, see Samuel A. Stoner, "Who is Descartes's Evil Genius?," *Journal of Early Modern Studies* 7 (2018): 9–29; and "The Moral Formation of Descartes's *Meditations*," *European Legacy* 27 (2022): 312–34.

[9] Descartes, *Meditations, Objections, and Replies*, 18. Significantly, Descartes likens the visible form of the piece of wax he is imagining to its clothing and his effort to distinguish the being of the wax from its visible form to "stripping" the wax of "its clothing" in order to "look at the wax in its nakedness" (Descartes, 18). In this way, Descartes casts his rejection of the link between the 'look' of a thing and its essential nature as a move away from the conventional, anthropomorphizing, and therefore deceptive way of thinking about nature characteristic of Aristotelian natural philosophy, toward a more natural and insightful form of science—a form of science that uncovers the truth of things rather than focusing on their deceptive appearances. It is unsurprising that Rousseau finds Descartes's procedure conducive to his attempt to see human beings "naked and without arms" (*SD*, 66). In this context, compare Jacob Klein's account of Aristotle's understanding of the connection between the visible appearance of a thing and its essential form in "Aristotle, an Introduction" in Jacob Klein, *Lectures and Essays*, eds. Robert B. Williamson and Elliott Zuckerman (Annapolis: St. John's College Press, 2013) to Richard Velkley's account of Rousseau's confrontation with Aristotle in Richard Velkley, *Being after Rousseau: Philosophy and Culture in Question* (Chicago: University of Chicago Press, 2002), 31–48.

Discourse on the Origin and Foundations of Inequality Among Men. While the Academy of Dijon asked about the origin of inequality and about whether inequality is authorized by natural law, Rousseau's title reveals his plan to address the Academy's question by illuminating the origin and the foundations of inequality among men. In conjunction with his decision to exclude any mention of natural law from his title, Rousseau's reference to foundations distinguishes the scope and content of the *Second Discourse* from the more limited and conventional concerns of the Academy. More precisely, Rousseau's search for foundations *replaces* the Academy's preoccupation with natural law. Rousseau follows Descartes in leaving behind the scholastic tradition in and through an effort to discover new foundations for human knowledge.

The latter point becomes explicit in the concluding paragraph of the Preface to the *Second Discourse*, which casts Rousseau's search for knowledge of human nature as an attempt to disclose the "unshakeable base" and "foundations" upon which "the edifice" of human society is raised (*SD*, 55–56). The allusion to the opening paragraph of Descartes's *Meditations* is unmistakable, and Rousseau's interest in foundations suggests that he is a follower of Descartes. If Descartes's search for foundational knowledge aims to uncover the principles that ground the stable edifice of scientific knowledge, however, Rousseau's search for foundational knowledge works to reveal the principles that govern the dynamic process of human history.

Though he begins by imagining the physical life of natural man, Rousseau's methodical doubt culminates in his investigation of "the metaphysical and moral side" of this primal being (*SD*, 71). Crucially, natural man's soul is characterized by freedom and perfectibility, but Rousseau emphasizes that these capacities exist in a state of pure potency in natural man. Not only have natural man's capacities not begun to develop, but they "could never develop by themselves" (*SD*, 89). Thus, Rousseau emphasizes the simplicity of natural man:

> His imagination portrays nothing to him; his heart asks nothing of him. His modest needs are so easily found at hand, and he is so far from the degree of knowledge necessary for desiring to acquire greater knowledge, that he can have neither foresight nor curiosity. The spectacle of nature becomes indifferent for him by dint of becoming familiar to him. There is always the same order, there are always the same revolutions. He does not have the mind to wonder at the greatest marvels, and it is not in him that one must seek the philosophy man needs in order to observe once what he has seen every day. His soul, which nothing agitates, gives itself over to the sole feeling of its present existence, without any idea of the future, however near it may be. (*SD*, 74)

The soul of natural man is unstirred, motionless, still. Though it is not empty, it is untroubled by thoughts about the future and the hopes, fears, desires, and passions such thoughts provoke. Natural man's soul is wholly present to itself. Though it possesses no image or idea of itself, it has a pure and immediate sense of self. If Descartes's *Meditations on First Philosophy* uncovers the *cogito*—the 'I think' that accompanies every thought, guarantees the irreducibility of subjectivity, and ensures that the self knows itself with absolute certainty—Rousseau's meditations on first humanity penetrate further into the depths of the human psyche, uncovering a primordial, pre-discursive, unreflective self-awareness that precedes and grounds all forms of self-consciousness and self-knowledge. If Descartes reasons, "I think, therefore

I am,"[10] Rousseau's concept of the sentiment of existence means: "I feel I am."

Rousseau's Critique of Descartes

Modern philosophy was born of a sense that reason was in crisis because classical philosophy and its medieval variants had failed in their efforts to provide clear, reliable, and effective guidance to human thought and action. On the level of theory, the unending disagreements that seemed to characterize scholastic disputations created doubts concerning reason's capacity to secure knowledge of the grounds and nature of reality. At the same time, increasingly detailed and precise observations of nature led to new developments in natural philosophy, which indicated that Aristotelian teleology and the Ptolemaic cosmologies it engendered were sources of error and illusion. On the level of practice, the rise of the medieval university gradually detached philosophy from ordinary moral and political life by casting it as an academic discipline. At the same time, increasingly spirited and public theological controversies enflamed anger and provoked sectarian violence across Europe. Reason seemed impotent and fruitless at best and deceptive and harmful at worst.

In response to these difficulties, the founders of modern philosophy sought to reconceive reason to ensure the success of its efforts to make scientific progress and promote human flourishing. Descartes exemplifies this movement of thought. Dissatisfied by his education, distressed by his ignorance, and displaced by the wars of religion ravaging Europe, Descartes formulates a new method of reasoning in an attempt to guarantee reason's discovery of truth in the sciences. Aware of human reason's tendency to generate and reinforce deceptive beliefs, however, and

[10] Descartes, *Discourse on Method*, 33.

conscious of the reasonableness of accepting merely probable but practically useful opinions, Descartes enacts a radical form of doubt in order to strip the mind of its attachment to common opinion, undermine its naïve trust that appearances reveal reality, and discover what, if anything, can be known with absolute certainty. Ultimately, Descartes's doubt leads him to ground scientific knowledge in the knowing subject's consciousness of its own thinking and in the content of the ideas that the knowing subject clearly and distinctly perceives in its own mind. Methodically applied, these innate ideas serve to organize the disordered material received through the senses, allowing the knower to describe intelligible processes with the utmost precision and to predict their outcome with incredible accuracy. The series of material and efficient causes that determine the processes that underly and explain natural phenomena becomes the principal object of scientific inquiry, and scientific knowledge makes it possible for us to interrupt, change, and control the natural processes that we understand. Descartes initiates a new beginning in philosophy that seeks to ensure that reason is a dependable source of clear, distinct, and useful knowledge.

Descartes's turn inward, away from the forms of worldly beings that appear to the senses and toward the self-conscious subject as the primal object of philosophical inquiry, sets the agenda for modern philosophy and for its investigations of the nature and significance of human knowledge. Rousseau positions the *Second Discourse* within this tradition of thought by appropriating a Cartesian mode of doubt in order to think behind deceptive appearances and traditional conceptions of the human being so as to discover the essence of the human. Like Descartes, Rousseau develops an account of subjectivity as the foundation of his account of human being. Unlike Descartes, though, Rousseau's description of the still soul of natural man denies the existence of ideas that are innate or natural to the human mind. On Rousseau's account, natural man is wholly absorbed by the "purely animal functions" of sensation and perception (*SD*, 73). And if Rousseau's claim that "every animal has ideas, since it has senses" indicates that natural man has ideas (*SD*, 71), it is crucial to emphasize that these ideas owe their origin and content to sensation alone—they are always only the concrete and simple ideas of the particular objects that are immediately present to natural man's senses.

This line of thought appears to follow Locke's criticism of the Cartesian doctrine of innate ideas, and Rousseau's account of the still soul of natural man echoes Locke's characterization of the human mind as a *tabula rasa* that is like "white paper" because it is "void of all characters" and "without any ideas."[11] Whereas Locke assumes that sensation and reflection are both natural to human beings, however, Rousseau denies that humans are reflective by nature. It might seem that Rousseau's claim that sensation is the sole source of natural man's ideas aligns him with Condillac, Helvétius, and other 'sensationist' critics of Locke.[12] Whereas the sensationists claim that sensation is both necessary and sufficient for human knowledge, however, Rousseau denies that the pure sensation characteristic of the still mind of natural man can generate thought, much less knowledge. The latter point is explicit in Rousseau's notes on Helvétius's *On the Mind*, which repeatedly stress that human thinking and knowing depend not only on the mind's receptivity to sense experience, but also on the mind's activity in grasping, comprehending, remembering, and

[11] John Locke, *An Essay Concerning Human Understanding* (New York: Prometheus Books, 1995), 59.

[12] For a helpful overview of the sensationist tradition, see John C. O'Neal, *The Authority of Experience: Sensationist Theory in the French Enlightenment* (University Park: Penn State University Press, 1996).

judging what it perceives through the senses.[13] This explains why, immediately after characterizing the still soul of natural man in the *Second Discourse*, Rousseau emphasizes that his account of natural man creates a seemingly unbridgeable gulf between "pure sensations" and even "the simplest knowledge" (*SD*, 74).

Ultimately, Rousseau's account of the still soul of natural man entails a radical critique of Descartes and his influence on the orientation and development of modern philosophy. Even as he affirms Descartes's rejection of classical and medieval thought and follows Descartes in questioning the ancients for their naïve faith in visible forms as expressions of the essences of the beings we encounter in the world, Rousseau reveals that Descartes and his followers are insufficiently rigorous in their efforts to uncover and question the premises of that tradition and that their thinking continues to be governed by unexamined but questionable assumptions they inherited from the tradition they seek to transcend. More specifically, Descartes and his followers assume the truth of a basically Aristotelian account of the human—either insofar as they assume that the human is an essentially rational being or insofar as they affirm that the human is naturally oriented toward knowledge. Descartes accepts as an unshakeable premise a conception of the human being derived from purported facts about the human mind he discovers through his experience of his own thinking, which leads him to conclude not only that the human is a thinking thing, but also that certain ideas that he encounters in his own mind are innate or natural to the human mind. Locke's experience of his own capacity to distinguish and combine ideas leads him to conclude that such reflection is

[13] See Rousseau's "Notes on Helvétius's *On the Mind*" in Jean-Jacques Rousseau, *Autobiographical, Scientific, Religious, Moral, and Literary Writings*, trans. Christopher Kelly (Hanover, NH: Dartmouth College Press, 2006), 204–12.

natural to the human mind. Finally, the sensationists' confidence that sensation alone is sufficient to account for the genesis of human knowledge is rooted in their confidence that humans are knowers by nature. Rousseau sees that Descartes and his followers have not questioned whether their most basic assumptions about the human being are true and have therefore failed to consider the possibility that thinking, reasoning, and knowing are unnatural and problematic activities.

Rousseau's Critique of Reason

Rousseau's critique of Descartes and his followers is rooted in his more comprehensive criticism of all prior attempts to clarify human nature and the foundations of human social and political life through an account of the state of nature. These attempts, Rousseau claims, have all been vitiated by the fact that they have "carried into the state of Nature ideas they had taken from society," such that "they spoke of savage man and they were depicting civil man" (*SD*, 62). At work, here, is a form of question begging in which a thinker seeking knowledge of human being assumes that certain capacities or characteristics they observe in themselves or others are permanent or natural features of the human condition without considering the possibility that these capacities or characteristics may be artificial effects of fundamental changes that humanity has undergone over time.

For Rousseau, this form of question begging about human nature is itself a product of the historical process. On Rousseau's account of human history, new material conditions cause psychological developments in natural man that lead him to forsake his solitary life of self-sufficiency and contentment to lead a social existence. Social existence breeds amour-propre, which leads each human being to prioritize themself and their own good above all. Amour-propre inclines human beings to attend to those features of the world that confirm ideas and theoretical frameworks that preserve or promote the state of affairs they most desire. Ultimately, this way of thinking generates a tendency to seek out "moral proof" of one's opinions by adducing "reasons for existing facts" that seem advantageous or desirable rather than attempting to ascertain "the real existence of these facts" and whether or not they are "established by nature" (*SD*, 143).

The passions precede and motivate human reasoning and distort our vision of the world. Reason's passionate efforts to justify facts that seem advantageous or desirable conceal the distortions wrought by passion. Reason is conditioned by the irrational, and ignorance of this crucial fact is the root and fruit of philosophy's search for truth. Simultaneously inspired and blinded by their desire for knowledge, the philosophers of the past unconsciously make unjustified assumptions about the naturalness of reason and the goodness of knowledge to justify their own activity. The belief in reason's goodness is the foundational prejudice of philosophy, and philosophy has been prejudiced and therefore unphilosophical since its inception.

Rousseau and the Historical Character of Knowledge

Rousseau's account of the still soul of natural man reveals that, contrary to the prejudice of the philosophers of the past, humans naturally lack the capacities to think, reason, and know. But, humans have developed these capacities. Rousseau's account of human being entails that knowledge is historical—triply so. First, the intellectual capacities that make knowledge possible and, a fortiori, knowledge itself emerge in and through human history.[14]

[14] This is a principal theme of part 2 of the *Second Discourse*, which traces the course of human history from the state of nature, to the primitive social orders that allowed for the invention of agriculture and metallurgy, to the fateful advent of property. This historical development arrives at a climax when,

Second, as human psychology develops, humans adopt new forms of social and political life such that the historical process generates new objects for human reflection and human knowledge advances in and through history. Third, knowledge of human nature ultimately depends on knowledge of the historical character of human thinking and knowing. One especially remarkable feature of the *Second Discourse* is that it tacitly suggests that Rousseau is the first thinker to comprehend the triply historical character of human knowledge and, by implication, the first philosopher to attain adequate knowledge of human nature. This point becomes especially clear in and through Rousseau's confrontation with Descartes. Though Rousseau's critique of Descartes is rooted in a more comprehensive critique of philosophical rationalism as such, the problems inherent in reason become particularly acute in the modern age in and through Descartes's thought.

Rousseau's critique of reason is rooted in his account of reason's historical character. The latter account reveals not only that humans are not naturally rational beings, but also that reason emerges after and because of the passions, that reason is subordinate to and governed by the passions, and that the development of reason excites the passions. Ultimately, reason's history reveals that reason generates and intensifies amour-propre and that amour-propre compels reason to undertake increasingly self-assertive forms of self-justification that cause it to overlook its own

following the invention of property, humanity's interest in, attachment to, and pursuit of property causes all humanity's intellectual capacities to emerge: "Here, then, are all our faculties developed, memory and imagination in play, pride involved, reason activated, and the mind having almost reached the extent of the perfection of which it is susceptible" (*SD*, 100). It is noteworthy that Rousseau qualifies his claim here—the mind has *almost* reached its proper perfection. Does the perfection of the mind require insight into human perfectibility and the historical character of the human being?

passionate, limited, and problematic character. On Rousseau's account, this dynamic is always already at work in human reason's quest for knowledge.[15]

Philosophy's prejudiced faith in the naturalness and goodness of reason is expressed in the Aristotelian dicta that humans are rational animals, that humans naturally desire to know, and that the noblest and best life is one devoted to the contemplation of the truths that reason discovers.[16] If he is critical of these traditional theses, however, Rousseau is attentive to the Platonic-Socratic emphasis on the primacy of perplexity and the role of knowledge of ignorance in and for philosophical thinking. Further, Rousseau praises the ancients for their understanding of the

[15] Cf. this striking condemnation of reason and philosophy from part 1 of the *Second Discourse*:

> It is reason that engenders pride, and it is reflection that fortifies it. It is reason that turns man back upon himself. It is reason that separates him from everything that bothers and afflicts him. It is philosophy that isolates him; it is by means of it that he secretly says at the sight of a suffering man: perish if you will, I am safe. No longer do anything but dangers of the entire society disturb the tranquil slumber of the philosopher and tear him from his bed. His fellow human being can have his throat slit with impunity beneath his window; he has only to put his hands over his ears and argue with himself a bit to keep nature, which rebels within him, from making him identify with the person being assassinated. (SD, 84–85)

[16] Aristotle himself seems to doubt that human beings can attain scientific knowledge of the whole, and he is aware that humans qua humans cannot live a purely contemplative life. See Aristotle, *Nicomachean Ethics*, 1177b27ff and Aristotle, *Metaphysics*, 982b29ff, and compare the latter passage both to Aristotle's account of slavery in book 1 of the *Politics* and to Rousseau's epigraph to the *Second Discourse*. The question of whether and to what extent Rousseau was aware of any doubts about the contemplative life that Aristotle may have entertained is beyond the scope of this essay. For present purposes, the important point is that the Aristotelian tradition has tended to overlook Aristotle's subtle qualifications of seemingly foundational theses.

difficulties that powerful passions create for human life and the need for well-ordered institutions that moderate and direct the passions toward noble ends. Taken together, such considerations begin to explain how Rousseau can hold up Socrates as an exemplary philosopher even as he praises Spartan accounts of moral and martial virtue. Despite his admiration for Socrates and Sparta, however, Rousseau's critique of reason accuses ancient philosophy of overlooking the fact that reason itself is always already the source of problematic passions. Accordingly, Rousseau concludes, the ancients are overly optimistic about reason's capacity to make progress—both in the individual's theoretical efforts to liberate themself from passionate attachment to convention and opinion for the sake of knowledge and in practical efforts of individuals and communities to govern the passions for the sake of virtue.[17]

For Rousseau, Descartes's thinking represents a decisive but problematic advance beyond the ancients. On one hand, Descartes's skeptical critique of the philosophical tradition leads him to reject traditional, teleological accounts of the human soul and lays the groundwork for his account of reason as "a universal instrument."[18] Rousseau joins Descartes in his critique of that tradition, and he follows Descartes, Hobbes, and other early

[17] For a more comprehensive development of this line of criticism, see Thomas L. Pangle, *The Life of Wisdom: Rousseau's* Reveries of a Solitary Walker (Ithaca, NY: Cornell University Press, 2023). The present essay's analysis of Rousseau's Cartesian rhetoric suggests that Rousseau may have been more alive to the centrality of Socratic knowledge of ignorance to philosophical thinking than Pangle's criticism allows. For a reading of the *Reveries* that casts Rousseau as a Socratic, see Laurence D. Cooper, *Dreaming of Justice, Waking to Wisdom: Rousseau's Philosophic Life* (Chicago: University of Chicago Press, 2023). For a treatment of the Platonic dimensions of Rousseau's thought, see David Lay Williams, *Rousseau's Platonic Enlightenment* (University Park: Penn State University Press, 2010).

[18] Descartes, *Discourse on Method*, 46.

modern thinkers in their accounts of reason's instrumental character. On the other hand, Descartes fails to question the naturalness of reason and posits that reason can provide itself with a method that guarantees its discovery of useful knowledge. Accordingly, Descartes exalts reason and emphasizes its beneficial effects. Indeed, a principal goal of Descartes's *Discourse on Method* is to articulate a new justification of reason's goodness through a rhetorical presentation of the new science as the vehicle of a revolutionary philanthropic enterprise that takes responsibility for humanity's fate and promotes the wellbeing of all human beings. If properly directed, reason is far more powerful and far better for human beings than the philosophers of the past had dared to hope. What initially appears to be a skeptical assault on the philosophical tradition comes to light as a spirited defense of this tradition's foundational prejudice.

In the context of Rousseau's critique of reason, Descartes's justification of reason is especially troubling—not simply because it expresses Descartes's failure to question the naturalness and goodness of reason, but also because it prevents Descartes from considering the possibility that reason is the source of the problems it seeks to overcome. For Rousseau, Descartes's defense of the new science as a source of human power serves to intensify amour-propre. Further, because Descartes's vision of the new science depends on his account of reason as an instrument of the passions and his affirmation of the goodness of the passionate quest to satisfy humanity's limitless desires, his justification of reason liberates and legitimates an unlimited amour-propre as the guiding principle of human thought and action. But, Rousseau sees amour-propre as the inspiration for "all the harm [humans] do to one another" (*SD*, 147). Accordingly, he cannot but conclude that Descartes's attempt to make reason more powerful is destined to generate increasingly profound forms of vanity, decadence and servitude.[19] At the same time, Descartes's rhetorical efforts to inspire widespread faith in and hope for the new science reinforce traditional assumptions about the naturalness and goodness of reason. Accordingly, Descartes's attempt to justify reason by empowering reason has the effect of multiplying and intensifying the problems that reason generates for human life while simultaneously concealing the fact that reason is the source of these problems. The history of reason is a story of the progress of reason, but the progress of reason ultimately only generates increasingly profound self-forgetfulness and increasingly incomprehensible forms of misery.

The latter dynamic serves as the immediate backdrop of Rousseau's critique of the sciences and the arts in the *First Discourse*. The progress of the sciences and the arts in the modern age and modernity's optimism about the power and goodness of reason seem to occasion Rousseau's insight into reason's historical and problematic character. Indeed, Rousseau testifies that his confrontation with modern scientific culture was the source of a transformative experience, akin to religious conversion, that revealed the tradition's faith in the naturalness and goodness of reason as a prejudice and culminated in a singular moment of insight into reason's historical and problematic character.[20] This insight, born of Rousseau's particular historical situation, is the foundational premise of his critique of reason and his subsequent

---

[19] In this context, it is fruitful to compare part six of Descartes's *Discourse on Method* to note nine of the *Second Discourse*. Whereas Descartes encourages humans to make themselves into "masters and possessors of nature" (Descartes, *Discourse on Method*, 49), Rousseau condemns the effort to make oneself into "the sole master of the universe" as an expression of an overweening and tyrannical amour-propre (*SD*, 129).

[20] See Jean-Jacques Rousseau, *The Confessions and Correspondence, Including the Letters to Malesherbes*, trans. Christopher Kelly (Hanover, NH: Dartmouth College Press, 1995), 294–95.

attempts to address the problem of reason.[21] For Rousseau, the philosophical tradition is plagued by profound self-ignorance, and his own critique of reason is a world-historical moment in and through which philosophy finally attains knowledge of its own nature. The historical process itself appears to be the source of Rousseau's insight into the historical character of reason and knowledge, and this insight seems to complete the history of reason's quest for self-knowledge. Rousseau's philosophy of history looks like the end of history for philosophy.

Rousseau on the Origin of Knowledge

Rousseau's account of the historical character of reason and knowledge raises the question of how reason and knowledge come to be. Rousseau takes up this question immediately following his description of the still soul of natural man, and he needs to take it up immediately after this description because the advent of the capacities to think and know establishes the formal cause that governs all further historical developments of the human being. But, accounting for the origin of knowledge proves difficult:

> The more one meditates on this subject, the more the distance from pure sensations to the simplest knowledge increases in our eyes; and it is impossible to conceive how a man, by his strength alone, without the aid of communication, and without the spur of necessity, could have bridged so great an interval. (*SD*, 74)

Rousseau occasionally suggests that 'new circumstances' are sufficient to initiate and explain human history, but he is explicit that the soul of natural man is so still that even "the greatest marvels" do not disturb its repose (*SD*, 74). New material conditions

---

[21] See Rousseau's letter to Malesherbes of January 12, 1762 in Rousseau, *The Confessions*, 574–77.

are necessary but insufficient to explain the genesis of human thinking and knowing, and Rousseau posits that the genesis of even the simplest knowledge requires "the aid of communication."

Rousseau develops the latter suggestion in a remarkable digression on the question of the origin of language. It is not immediately clear what Rousseau thinks the 'simplest knowledge' consists in, but his first reference to knowledge in the digression on language suggests that it involves understanding the properties of a particular object and what distinguishes this object from other objects such that one can identify it as a specific type of object: 'that is a tree' (*SD*, 78). Such knowledge requires a 'general idea' (tree), an image or representation of a particular being perceived through the senses (that thing over there), and a judgment that subsumes the particular under the general, categorizing it as an instance of the archetype (that thing over there is this kind of thing: tree). But, Rousseau emphasizes, the sort of "abstractions" required to form a general idea are "difficult and not particularly natural mental operations" (*SD*, 78). Further, general ideas as such can be "conceived of only through discourse" because they can only be understood and grasped in terms of "definitions" (*SD*, 78–79). "Hence, one has to state propositions, hence one has to speak in order to have general ideas" (*SD*, 79). Indeed, "general ideas can enter the mind only with the help of words, and the understanding grasps them only by means of propositions" (*SD*, 79).

The claim here is not that words cause general ideas or that propositions and definitions generate knowledge, but rather that knowing is always already a form of discursive thinking that is, by its very nature, conceptual, propositional, linguistic. General ideas are but unspoken words articulated in thought, and the mind grasps the connection between concepts through judgments that constitute propositions or sentences. When Rousseau claims that the simplest knowledge requires the help of communication, then, he does not mean that communication is a chronologically prior efficient cause of knowledge, but rather that human thinking and knowing are linguistic in form. They are in essence if not in actuality modes of communication.[22]

As striking as it is to see Rousseau developing some of the core premises of the so-called linguistic turn in philosophy, it is crucial to note that his linguistic account of human knowledge generates difficulties. To explain the origin of human knowledge, it is necessary to explain the origin of human thinking and speaking. The latter two capacities are inseparable, but their inseparability creates a perplexity about priority: "for if Men needed speech in order to learn how to think, they needed even more to know how to think in order to find the art of speech" (*SD*, 77). But, the still soul of natural man makes it impossible for him to develop thought or speech for himself. Natural man could only become capable of thinking and speaking were he taught how to think and speak by a thinking and speaking being. But, Rousseau's account of the natural man's still soul entails that he is incapable of learning, and Rousseau's description of the pure state of nature seems to rule out the existence of a being who could teach natural man to think or speak. Thus, Rousseau despairs of the possibility of knowing the origin of language:

---

[22] For an account of the origins, genesis, and significance of this way of understanding the connection between language, thought, and knowledge, see Charles Taylor, *The Language Animal: The Full Shape of the Human Linguistic Capacity* (Cambridge: Belknap Press, 2016). Taylor foregrounds Herder's articulation of insights that Rousseau had already begun to develop in the *Second Discourse* and the *Essay on the Origin of Languages*, but he does not dwell on Rousseau's significance for or influence on Herder.

> As for myself, frightened by the multiplying difficulties and convinced of the almost demonstrated impossibility that languages could have arisen and been established by purely human means, I leave to anyone who should wish to undertake it the examination of this difficult problem: Which was the more necessary, an already formed society for the institution of languages or already invented languages for the establishment of society? (*SD*, 80)

As it is with language, so it is with thought, reason, and knowledge. Rousseau initiates his digression on the origin of language to explain the origin of thinking and knowing, but his attempt to explain the origin of language reveals that it is impossible to explain the origin of thinking and knowing.

Conclusion

The *Second Discourse* pursues knowledge of the human through a methodical doubt that strips thinking of its attachment to traditional concepts and its faith in the reliability of appearances. This doubt culminates in Rousseau's description of the still soul of natural man. But, immediately after describing natural man's still soul, Rousseau shows that adopting this description as an account of the essence of the human makes it simultaneously necessary and impossible to explain the genesis of human thinking and knowing. In this way, Rousseau indicates that the natural man he describes in the *Second Discourse* cannot serve as the foundation of human history and calls into question the stability of the foundational principle he claims to establish.

The action of Rousseau's argument suggests that he emphasizes the foundational character of his description of natural man in order to call its foundational character into question. Rousseau does this through an investigation of the origin and conditions of human knowledge. Rousseau's account of the problem of human knowledge shows that his own claim to know the human is problematic. The problematic character of Rousseau's claim to knowledge of the human reveals the inadequacy of his meditations on first humanity. Rousseau's imitation of Descartes's search for foundational knowledge illuminates the problematic character of Descartes's foundationalism.

Passionate prejudice always threatens to enslave reason and make philosophy dogmatic. But, a radical doubt that repudiates all prejudice as falsehood threatens to strip humans of all humanity by alienating them from themselves and their history. Aware that radical doubt is a useful way to "destroy" "ancient errors and inveterate prejudices" (*SD*, 88), Rousseau adopts this way of thinking, but not without suggesting its limits. This fact illuminates an overarching rhetorical conceit of the *Second Discourse*. Rousseau enacts a will to foundational knowledge in order to show the will to foundational knowledge undermining itself. He engages and provokes his reader's hope for certain knowledge to puncture and deflate this hope. He takes advantage of the prejudices of philosophic rationalism in order to reorient human thinking, turning it away from its natural, spirited demands for definition and certainty, toward an awareness of the perplexities that the search for knowledge uncovers.

Rousseau's description of the still soul of natural man points beyond itself to the problem of human knowledge. Thinking through the problem of human knowledge in the *Second Discourse* leads toward knowledge of the problematic character of human thinking. Like Descartes, Rousseau seeks to initiate a new beginning for philosophy. By following Descartes's quest for foundational knowledge to its logical conclusion, however, Rousseau discloses the problematic character of this quest. Philosophy must abandon the attempt to settle thought on firm foundations because philosophizing always unsettles thought by making it attentive to its own questionable character.[23]

[23] This conclusion complements other interpretations of the *Second Discourse* that call the intention of Rousseau's account of natural man and the possibility of the pure state of nature into question. See Michael Davis, *The Autobiography of Philosophy: Rousseau's* The Reveries of the Solitary Walker (Lanham, MD: Rowman & Littlefield, 1999); Velkley, *Being after Rousseau*; Jonathan Marks, *Perfection and Harmony in the Thought of Jean-Jacques Rousseau* (Cambridge: Cambridge University Press, 2005); Denise Schaeffer, *Rousseau on Education, Freedom, and Judgment* (University Park: Penn State University Press, 2013), all of which have made important contributions to my own thinking about Rousseau, his manner of writing, his understanding of human nature, and his mode of philosophizing. I am grateful to Rachel Coleman, Derek Duplessie, Matt Dinan, Michael Matraia, Veronica Ogle, Richard Velkley, the participants in the 2023 A.V. Elliott Conference on Great Books and Ideas at Mercer University, and several excellent students in my "Individual and Community" class at Assumption University in Spring 2023 for conversations, criticisms, questions, and suggestions about the line of thought developed in this essay.

5.

SINCERITY AND SELF-DECEPTION IN *THE PROFESSION OF FAITH OF THE SAVOYARD VICAR*

John Warner

Early modern philosophers viewed the problem of self-deception as one of overriding moral, epistemological, and political importance, and Rousseau's analysis of this problem is widely recognized to be among the most penetrating of his—or any—era. Indeed, whether it is the cunning *l'homme du monde* who conceals his self-interest by lowering a "deceitful veil of civility," the philosopher who puts "his hands over his ears and argue[s] with himself a bit" in order to ignore the sounds of suffering, the self-satisfied theatergoer who in "bad faith" defends the very institution which is corrupting him, or the alienated "bourgeois" suspended helplessly between the poles of independence and sociability, we find in Rousseau an unusually comprehensive account both of the varieties of self-deceptive behavior and the mental gymnastics that self-deceivers deploy just to get through the day.

Though Rousseau is certainly not the only philosopher to criticize self-deception, the intensity of his criticism—coupled with his enthusiastic praise of simplicity and uprightness—has led many interpreters to view him as an advocate of simple-souled sincerity and an opponent of dishonesty and dissimulation in all its guises.[1] Though this reading is illuminating in many respects, it neglects the highly significant point that Rousseau's *exemplars* as well as his villains appear to be engaged in something like self-deception. When, for instance, we consider the extent to which Emile and Saint-Preux are captive to illusions of their own making[2] and that even the virtuous Julie appears to engage in self-deception as a way of allaying her anxiety,[3] we are forced to wonder whether Rousseau was indeed so unreservedly critical of self-deception and whether it might be necessary to reexamine the role that this fraught concept plays in his work.

In what follows, I seek to contribute to this reexamination by analyzing *The Profession of Faith of the Savoyard Vicar* and arguing that yet another of Rousseau's exemplars—the vicar himself—is engaged in self-deception. I make this general argument in three steps. First, I focus on the prologue to *The Profession* and show that the vicar is engaged in motivated irrationality, attending in particular to the way that the epistemically irrelevant desires for *self-esteem* and *epistemic closure* bias his inquiry and reveal some fairly galling shortcomings of self-knowledge. Second, I examine the vicar's understanding of the belief-adoption process and argue that it is designed specifically to beat back the demons of doubt rather than to discover truth. Specifically, I show not

---

[1] Jason Neidleman, *Rousseau's Ethics of Truth: A Sublime Science of Simple Souls* (New York: Routledge, 2016); Ruth Grant, *Hypocrisy and Integrity* (Chicago: University of Chicago Press, 2008); Arthur Melzer, "Rousseau and the Modern Cult of Sincerity," in *The Legacy of Rousseau*, ed. Clifford Orwin and Nathan Tarcov (Chicago: University of Chicago Press), 274–95; Arthur Melzer, "The Origin of Counter-Enlightenment: Rousseau and the Cult of Sincerity," *American Political Science Review* 90, no. 2 (August 1996): 344–60.

[2] Matthew Maguire, *The Conversion of Imagination* (Cambridge: Harvard University Press, 2006).

[3] John Warner, "'I Know Not if I Deceive Myself': Rousseau's *Julie* and the Ambiguities of Self-Deception," *Journal of Politics* 84, no. 3 (July 2022): 1570–80.

only that the vicar elides the processes of sensing and judging in order to confer an unjustified feeling of certainty upon his beliefs, but that he does so *knowingly and intentionally*. Thus the vicar does not, as he claims, adopt beliefs that he cannot conceive of doubting; instead, he disingenuously fabricates feelings of certainty and attaches them to the beliefs he would *like* to be true. Finally, I show how the vicar's commitment to sincerity consummates his self-deceptive project. By reading the virtue of sincerity into his character, he is able to quietly ignore the problems with his view or to excuse them as the good-faith errors of a well-intentioned truth-seeker.

This argument, if successful, is significant in at least two respects. First, it presents a fundamental challenge to conventional readings of *The Profession*, which not only take the vicar's invocations of sincerity at face value but also claim that his commitments are in fact Rousseau's own.[4] If the vicar is indeed engaged in self-deception then he is surely not the exemplar of sincerity that he is said to be, and if Rousseau wrote the character of the vicar as a self-deceiver then there is strong reason to believe that his own views are not identical to the vicar's. I should add that, while I am not the first to raise questions about the purity of the

[4] Robin Douglass, *Rousseau and Hobbes: Nature, Free Will, and the Passions* (Oxford: Oxford University Press, 2015); Lee MacLean, *The Free Animal: Rousseau on Free Will and Human Nature* (Toronto: University of Toronto Press, 2013); David Williams, *Rousseau's Platonic Enlightenment* (University Park: The Pennsylvania State University Press, 2007); Peter Emberley, "Rousseau versus the Savoyard Vicar: The Profession of Faith Reconsidered," *Interpretation* 14, no. 2–3 (July 1986): 299–330; Henri Gouhier, *Les meditations métaphysiques de Jean-Jacques Rousseau* (Paris: Vrin, 1970); Morris Dickstein, "The Faith of a Vicar: Reason and Morality in Rousseau's Religion," *Yale French Studies* 28 (1961): 48–54; Ronald Grimsley, *Rousseau and the Religious Quest* (Oxford: Clarendon Press, 1968).

vicar's motives,[5] I am the first to ascribe to him an intention to self-deceive. The matter is highly significant both because the vicar himself puts such stress on his own intellectual and moral integrity and because most readers of *The Profession* still more or less accept his self-interpretation as authoritative (*E*, 266).[6] Second, it calls for a reexamination of the role that self-deception plays in Rousseau's own work. I have already noted that Rousseau is usually read as an uncompromising critic of self-deception, and though there is no denying that he is concerned about the psychological and social effects of self-deceptive activity, my argument suggests that he is also receptive to its potential benefits.

He Can't Handle the Truth: The Vicar's Sincerity Reconsidered

The Profession is a statement of religious belief delivered by an obscure country vicar to a disillusioned adolescent boy on the verge of a sexual awakening and suffering from a crisis of faith. It develops a providentially ordered conception of the universe with humanity at its center and has the intrinsically practical purpose of reinvigorating the religious and moral convictions of its audience(s). The work is divided into two parts: the first contains a design-based deistic argument which constitutes the vicar's own religious teaching, and the second develops a general critique of revealed religion and many of the "irrational" beliefs (e.g., in miracles) associated with it. These two sections are separated by a brief exchange between the vicar and his listener in which the

---

[5] John Scott, *Rousseau's God* (Chicago: University of Chicago Press, 2023), 144; Jennifer Einspahr, "The Beginning that Never Was: Mediation and Freedom in Rousseau's Political Thought," *Review of Politics* 72, no. 3 (Summer 2010): 437–61; Melzer, "Origin," 354.

[6] *E*, cited by page, refers to Rousseau's *Emile*, trans. Allan Bloom (New York: Basic Books, 1979).

latter observes that the former's positive doctrine, while not unappealing, is nonetheless subject to "a multitude of objections" (*E*, 294). By emphasizing the ambivalence of the adolescent boy's response, the author of *The Profession* suggests that the vicar's teaching may be problematic in important respects and thus invites the work's *other* audience—the reader of Rousseau's *Emile*—to reflect on what those problems might be.[7]

It is in this context that I want to focus on the way in which the vicar's interpretation of his own truth-seeking motives and to suggest that it is seriously, and systematically, deficient. In emphasizing the importance of the links between motivation and belief I follow the lead of the vicar himself, whose entire account of truth-seeking is founded on the premise of his sincerity and good faith. On this point, he begins *The Profession* by invoking these very qualities—"I am not a great philosopher…[but] I always love the truth…. If I am mistaken, it is in good faith"—and founding his credibility as a truth-seeker upon them: "taking the love of truth as my whole philosophy…I am resolved to accept as evident all knowledge to which in the sincerity of my heart I cannot refuse my consent." Here and elsewhere, the vicar suggests that his belief system should be taken seriously not because he is brilliant or well-credentialed but rather because his truth-seeking efforts are guided by the best intentions. To this end, the reader is repeatedly assured that the vicar has no ulterior motives for inquiring after the truth, that he seeks it for its own sake and will follow it wherever it may lead. Thus for the vicar it is his purity of will, along with a certain introspective perceptiveness which allows him to access his deeper-lying motivations, that ultimately authorizes his truth-telling mission (*E*, 266, 269–70).

[7] Rousseau draws explicit attention to the fact that *The Profession* has multiple audiences in a note, suggesting there that the vicar's speech should be helpful to all of them (see *E*, 295n).

Though the vicar begins *The Profession* by suggesting that his inquiry is motivated purely by truth-related interests, he quickly acknowledges that other and more practical considerations played an important role in motivating his quest for knowledge. On this score, it is significant to note that the teaching of *The Profession* is explicitly framed as a solution to the problem of *happiness* rather than that of truth:

> 'Oh, what sad pictures!' I [the adolescent boy] cried out with bitterness. 'If one must turn away from everything, what was the use for us of being born? And if one must despise happiness itself, *who knows how to be happy?' 'I do,' answered the priest* in a tone which struck me....Thereupon he made me understand that after having received my confessions he wanted to make me his. 'I shall unbosom all the sentiments of my heart to you,' he said, embracing me. *'You shall see me, if not as I am, then at least as I see myself....When you know well the state of my heart, you will know why I esteem myself happy."* (*E*, 266, emphasis added)

From the outset, *The Profession* makes plain that neither the vicar nor his listener are interested in the truth for its own sake. To the contrary, the only reason they are engaged in rational reflection at all is because their prospects for self-esteem and happiness depend on their doing so (see also *E*, 266, 270, 283–84; *SD* 73, 82).[8] In and of itself, this need not be epistemically problematic—everyone has *some* reason to pursue the truth, after all—but it does invite the reader to wonder whether the vicar's love of truth is strong enough to win out over his nontruth-related

[8] *SD*, cited by page, refers to the *Second Discourse* or *Discourse on the Origins of Inequality*, in Rousseau, *The Major Political Writings of Jean-Jacques Rousseau*, trans. John T. Scott (Chicago, University of Chicago Press, 2012).

interests *if and when* the two happen to conflict. On this point, Jason Neidleman has provocatively argued that Rousseau (and by extension, the vicar) effectively integrate the requirements of truth and happiness such that it would be impossible "to hold a belief that is both false and supportive of…happiness."[9] Yet in the passage above (and elsewhere, see, e.g., *E*, 294), the vicar explicitly acknowledges a distinction between truth and happiness when he observes that his profession advances a view of the world—and of himself—that may well be false but is nonetheless not open to revision because it so effectively advances his interest in self-esteem. Far from eliding truth and happiness, then, the text of *The Profession* emphasizes the possibility for conflict between the two.

Once we confront this possibility squarely, we quickly discover that the vicar not only does not love the truth for its own sake but is willing to sacrifice its demands where doing so advances his interest in happiness. Ironically, this tendency is most pronounced in the moments immediately after he reassures his audience that his truth-seeking is guided by "good faith." He follows this invocation of sincerity by confessing that he had broken his vow of celibacy multiple times and had impregnated at least one parishioner during his career as a priest. This disclosure, however, is not accompanied by the candid admission of wrongdoing which we would expect from a friend of the truth but rather by a wildly unconvincing attempt at self-justification:

> I know by my experience that conscience persists in following the order of nature against all the laws of men. We may very well be forbidden this or that, but remorse always reproaches us feebly for what well-ordered nature permits us….From my youth on I have respected

[9] Neidleman, *Sublime Science*, 7.

> marriage as the first and the holiest institution of nature. Having taken away my right to submit myself to it, I resolved not to profane it....This resolve is precisely what destroyed me. My respect for the bed of others left my faults exposed. The scandal had to be expiated. Arrested, interdicted, driven out, I was far more the victim of my scruples than of my incontinence. (*E*, 267)

The vicar's case is transparently disingenuous. He interprets his preference for young women as proof of his respect for marriage and feels no scruple about helping himself to what he self-interestedly believes is permitted by "well-ordered nature." He shows no concern about having broken a vow that he voluntarily took and, though fond of waxing lyrical about the glories of virtue, does not so much as pause to consider the fates of the women and child(ren) that he abandoned.[10] The interests of others do not even enter his calculus as he congratulates himself for abstaining from intercourse with married women and, in an astonishing turn, he manages to turn *himself* into the victim of the scandal which he himself created: "[a] few such experiences lead a reflective mind a long way. Seeing all the ideas that I had of the just, the decent, and all the duties of man overturned by gloomy

[10] The vicar's apathy at having abandoned the child(ren) he fathered contrasts sharply with the acute feelings of remorse that Rousseau himself repeatedly reports having after leaving his five children at a foundling home. In a letter to Mme. De Luxembourg, for instance, Rousseau says that the "self-reproach which my neglectful behavior has aroused in me has disturbed my peace of mind," and early in *Emile* (49) he writes that "he who cannot fulfill the duties of a father has no right to become one....Readers, you can believe me. I predict to whoever...neglects such holy duties that he will long shed bitter tears for his offense and will never find consolation for it." Without denying the obviously problematic nature of Rousseau's own paternity, we may at least say that he recognized his wrongdoing and that that recognition caused him considerable moral distress. This itself serves to distinguish him from the vicar, whose conscience reproached him only "feebly" for his actions.

observations, I lost each day one of the opinions I had received" (E, 267). The vicar chooses to view the disapproval which he so richly deserves as a form of unjust persecution and notes that the disenchantment it caused is what undermined his faith in God and the existence of a universal moral order. His descent into existential despair thus grows directly out of his inability to come to terms with and take responsibility for his moral failings.[11] He would sooner doubt God's providence than his own rectitude.

In all this disingenuous huffing and puffing we glimpse the vicar's broad willingness, as well as his extraordinary capacity, to distort reality where it suits his interests to do so. He demonstrates a kind of constitutive inability to acknowledge truths that are inconsistent with his self-image or might threaten his happiness, preferring instead to ignore or deny any evidence which could undermine the belief he has in his own virtue. To this end, we find him interpreting his behavior in implausible and highly selective ways, both ignoring considerations to which he ought to attend (e.g., "should I feel bad for abandoning those women and children?") and attending to considerations which he ought to ignore ("think of the women I *didn't* sleep with!," "what the other priests did was much worse!," etc.). The intelligent selectivity of

---

[11] It is worth noting that, later in *The Profession*, the vicar seems to admit that his sexual irresponsibility points to a character flaw but once again finds a scapegoat, this time his "mortal body:" "These illusions [about sex] have lasted too long for me. Alas, I recognized them too late and have been unable to destroy them completely. They will last as long as the mortal body which causes them. At least, although they may very well seduce me, they no longer deceive me. I know them for what they are; in following them, I despise them....I aspire to the moment when, after being delivered from the shackles of the body, I shall be *me* without contradiction or division" (*E*, 292). The vicar has found in metaphysical dualism a new means of excusing his sexual recklessness. By separating his spiritual human essence from his "mortal body" he also separates himself from his promiscuity—sex is something he does, but it is not who he is.

the vicar's errors—the fact that they relentlessly track the interests which motivated his inquiry in the first place—suggest that his failure of self-knowledge is in some way willful and that the very sincerity which was supposed to protect him from illusion is *itself* a kind of illusion which prevents him from having to acknowledge failings which would diminish his self-image.[12]

There is, of course, the possibility that the vicar is not engaged in self-deception at all but has instead been innocently led astray by his own biases. There are some prima facie reasons in support of this view: Rousseau himself acknowledges that errors of this kind are likely when doing something as difficult as interpreting one's own mental states—*especially* where religious questions are concerned (see, e.g., *R*, 72–73)[14]—and the vicar himself repeatedly acknowledges his fallibility (*E*, 268–69, 277, 294). Yet there are in the vicar's apologia a combination of features that lead us to suspect that the vicar's misinterpretation of his motives cannot be dismissed as good-faith mistakes. The first is that his errors are so obvious that it is difficult to explain how an intelligent person could fall prey to them without appealing to something like self-deception. On this point, it is important to acknowledge that the vicar is a perceptive and sympathetic

[12] One might object to this interpretation on the ground that admitting to an isolated error should not meaningfully diminish the vicar's self-esteem—no one is perfect, after all. But on this very point it is important to note that the vicar's error is hardly isolated: in his apologia he refers to "*a few* such experiences" and later indicates that he had never reformed his behavior (*E*, 293). The text itself thus points to the vicar's long history of sexual recklessness, thereby suggesting that it would be difficult indeed for him to fully reckon with his past actions without also being forced to qualify his virtuous self-image.

[14] *R*, cited by page number, refers to Rousseau's *The Reveries of the Solitary Walker, Botanical Writings, and Letter to Franquieres* in *Collected Writings of Rousseau*, ed. Christopher Kelly and Eve Grace, trans. Christopher Kelly and Judith R. Bush, vol. 8 (Hanover, NH: Dartmouth College Press, 2000).

character who demonstrates an ability to reason in a creative, subtle, and persuasive way about matters of profound complexity. Yet the case he makes in defense of his sexual practices is so outrageously unconvincing, so grotesquely lacking in credibility or seriousness, that one wonders how any rational being could articulate it with a straight face. It seems difficult to account for the disparity between the vicar's generalized rational competence and his local rational failings *without* invoking self-deception.

Second, his errors are *systematically related* in ways that advance fundamental interests which have nothing to do with truth. Those seeking to learn the truth about anything might, in principle, make all kinds of mistakes, and if one's errors were indeed sincere then we might expect them to be more or less randomly distributed across epistemic space.[15] In the interpretation of his own mental phenomena, however, the vicar's mistakes almost perfectly align with the (explicitly articulated) interest he has in maintaining his self-esteem. Thus the intelligent selectivity of the vicar's errors—the fact that they almost perfectly track his nontruth-related interests—is yet another strong reason to believe that they are not innocently motivated.[16]

Finally, and most revealingly, the vicar is not passive but *active* in the maintenance of his false beliefs. If we wanted to defend him against the charge of self-deception, we might argue that, however ill-considered or motivated his beliefs appear to be, he cannot be guilty of deceiving himself unless he is on some level aware of the problems with his view. Many people, after all, hold

---

[15] Rousseau himself makes an argument like this in book 2, chapter 3 of the *Social Contract* where he seeks to explain how the general will can be unerring although individual citizens will inevitably make erroneous judgments about what the common good requires.

[16] Herbert Fingarette, "Self-Deception Needs No Explaining," *The Philosophical Quarterly* 48, no. 192 (July 1998): 289–301.

wildly implausible beliefs simply because they have failed to thoroughly consider the matter or properly examine the evidence which bears on it. The vicar, however, cannot claim to be unaware of the potential problems with his behavior—indeed, he is acutely aware of them—and it is precisely this awareness which forces him to re-interpret events in a way that reconciles the apparent discrepancy between his conduct and his self-image. To this end, he engages his rational faculties in ways that maintain his strained view of reality: he executes, often quite creatively, many of the cognitive tasks which we associate with truth-seeking—he adduces reasons, he weighs evidence, he evaluates alternative possibilities, and so on—but does so in an obtuse and inevitably self-serving way. The vicar's readiness to use his critical reflectivity in the service of absurdity, to defend the indefensible, suggests that his epistemic failures cannot be viewed as good faith errors or even as products of laziness but rather as the result of a kind of willful misuse of his rational faculties. Indeed, as we watch him develop arguments in defense of his behavior, we have the distinct impression of someone doing a drunken impersonation of a rational being. The odd combination of critical reflectivity and epistemic recklessness which the vicar exhibits in his attempts at self-exculpation is, as Dion Scott-Kakures notes, perhaps the clearest indicator of self-deception: "in self-deception cognition is shaped by interests and desires even while the subject reasons critically and reflectively, taking herself to shape her attitudes in accord with her epistemic evaluations."[17]

Though it is hopefully now evident that the vicar's belief in his own love of truth is brought about, or at least maintained, via self-deception, I hasten to add that the desire for happiness is not

---

[17] Dion Scott-Kakures, "At 'Permanent Risk:' Reasoning and Self-Knowledge in Self-Deception," *Philosophy and Phenomenological Research* 65, no. 3 (July 2002): 586.

the only epistemically problematic motivation underwriting his inquiry. He also shows extreme sensitivity to the anxiety produced by uncertainty, asserting that the state of "uncertainty and doubt" about "the things it is important for us to know" is "painful" and is "too violent a state" to remain in for long: "I have never led a life so constantly disagreeable as during those times of perplexity and anxiety, when I ceaselessly wandered from doubt to doubt and brought back...only uncertainty, obscurity, and contradictions about the cause of my being and the principle of my duties." Though the vicar is relatively relaxed about his inability to resolve speculative metaphysical questions—on these issues, at least, he is happy to remain in "profound ignorance"—his anxiety with respect to moral and ethical questions which are "useful for practice" is so acute as to be intolerable. In fact, he finds the lack of absolute moral certainty so psychologically harmful as to require an intellectual system which can "produce conviction *immediately*" (*E*, 267–68, emphasis added).

It is not difficult to see how the fretful need to secure certainty *right now* might problematize one's truth-seeking endeavors, but the vicar, warmed by the conviction of his own truthfulness, does not pause to consider such difficulties as he characterizes his quest for truth in the most attractive possible light: "I was in that frame of mind of uncertainty and doubt which Descartes demands for the quest for truth. This state is hardly made to last. It is disturbing and painful. It is only the self-interest of vice or laziness of soul that keeps us in it. My heart was not sufficiently corrupted to enjoy myself in it" (*E*, 267). The vicar is once again very generous in his self-interpretation, first comparing his love of truth to that of Descartes and going on to view his eagerness to believe not as an example of wishful thinking but rather as a manifestation of inner goodness. Meanwhile he goes on to ascribe to non-believers the most sinister possible motives, arguing that agnosticism is motivated either by love of vice or "laziness of soul." This interpretation is as unpersuasive as it is ungenerous, for if the psychological weight of uncertainty is as heavy as the vicar says then it is not clear why a lazy agnostic would voluntarily elect to carry it. Thus it seems that the vicar is once again telling himself a pleasing but implausibly optimistic story about the relative purity of his truth-seeking motives in order to bolster his virtuous self-image.

Here as with the vicar's defense of his sexual practices, we see all the signs of self-deception. The self-righteousness, selective opacity, and motivated (ir)rationality all suggest that the vicar is not searching for the truth in good faith but is rather trying to backwards engineer a justification for a set of pre-determined conclusions which evidence does not necessarily support. Yet on the vicar's view, it is not he but his intellectual opponents—the "skeptic philosophers"—who are deceiving themselves: "these skeptic philosophers either do not exist or are the unhappiest of men. Doubt about the things it is important for us to know is too violent a state for the human mind, which does not hold out in this state for long. It decides in spite of itself one way or the other and prefers to be deceived rather than believe in nothing" (*E*, 268). The vicar claims that the mind naturally defaults toward belief rather than doubt and openly acknowledges that this natural tendency might lead to false or wishful believing. Yet he also claims that such believing is better than non-belief, which is psychologically perverse to the point of being impossible. It is on this epistemological basis that he builds his case against the skeptic: since one's mind decides "in spite of itself one way or another," those who claim to be agnostic are likely just atheists who do not realize it. And just as the skeptic is deceived about the forces underwriting his own doxastic activity, so too is he deceived about his reasons for seeking the truth: his examination of fundamental religious and moral questions is motivated not by love of truth but by pride, and so debates about God and morality are for him not serious practical matters but rather are just so many more opportunities to put his intellectual virtuosity on display. Philosophy is thus reduced to a kind of parlor game rather than being a genuine search for truth (see, e.g., *E*, 268–69). Crucially, however, the skeptic himself fails to realize this: he is taken in by his own performance and mistakes his philosophical peacocking and showy contrarianism for serious truth-seeking. It is in *this* way that he falls into self-deception, for he (willfully and to some degree deliberately) misinterprets his own agnostic posturing as evidence of his commitment to truth rather than an expression of his desire to shine in the eyes of others.

The vicar's critique of the skeptic's inner-life is fascinating and to some degree plausible—his nimble navigation of the mind's dark corners suggests deep familiarity with self-deceptive technique—but it exhibits the same self-deceptive practices we have already seen. One notes, first, the self-servingly biased character of his case: the vicar never misses an opportunity to praise himself, and here he flatteringly compares his love of truth to that of Descartes. To sustain this comparison and the sense of self-worth which it protects, however, the vicar must once again distort reality in some fairly basic ways, for though he seems to take Descartes's example to reveal the "disturbing and painful" nature of uncertainty it in fact points to precisely the opposite conclusion. As Pierre Masson points out in his searching interpretation of *The Profession*, Descartes was actually quite comfortable with the experience of doubt, living in uncertainty about a number of central philosophical questions for a full nine years.[18] Far, then, from suggesting that the lack of certainty is an unpleasant

[18] Pierre-Maurice Masson, *La Religion de J.J. Rousseau* (Paris: Hachette, 1916), 2:86.

condition which truth-seekers should flee as quickly as possible, Descartes's case points instead to the opposite conclusion that anyone with an interest in truth must learn to become comfortable with *not* knowing.

In this context, it is important to emphasize that the vicar, unlike Descartes, is uninterested in speculation for its own sake and seeks certainty only with respect to questions that are "useful for practice" (*E*, 269). Hilail Gildin claims that the practical orientation of the vicar's inquiry helps to justify his desire for *immediate* certainty, for if the end of belief is to orient action then one must necessarily proceed as if certain things are true: "the vicar could reply [to Descartes] that, given his situation…waiting is simply out of the question. The questions Descartes puts off for later…must be faced immediately."[19] But surely the fact that Descartes is content to put moral and religious questions "off for later" shows that "waiting" isn't at all "out of the question" and that uncertainty—whether experienced in the practical or theoretical realm—is not *necessarily* attended by the fretful anxiety which the vicar ascribes to it. The vicar's invocation of Descartes thus serves only to highlight the problems with his own account: it undermines his effort to characterize his personal discomfort with uncertainty as an immutable feature of the human mind and shows him to have fabricated an unnecessary need to believe *now* in order to conceal the dubiousness of his belief-adoption procedure. And here as before, the vicar's distortions and exaggerations are simply too purposive, too systemically linked to the advancement of nontruth-related interests, to be characterized as good faith mistakes: by indulging the fiction that he resembles a great philosopher, the vicar manages to preserve his self-esteem, and

[19] Hilail Gildin, "On Rousseau's Confession of Faith of the Savoyard Vicar," *Interpretation* 43, no.2 (Winter 2017): 204–5.

by passing off his desire for epistemic closure as a love of knowledge he deceives himself about his own truthfulness.

The vicar's broader criticism of skeptical philosophers also shows evidence of self-deception. Though his case against the skeptic has some plausibility and suggests that he has a sophisticated understanding of belief-formation processes (a point I shall return to in the following section), it nonetheless serves a self-deceptive function. On this point, consider that the vicar initiates his attack on the motives of philosophers immediately after claiming that he finds the experience of uncertainty emotionally intolerable. This shift of emphasis is very abrupt and requires explanation. It certainly serves to discredit his opponents, which will make his own alternative appear more attractive by default, but more important is the way that his sudden focus on others' truth-seeking motives serves to draw attention away from his own. The vicar never answers or even acknowledges the obvious question of whether his desire for certainty might lead him to adopt certain beliefs prematurely, but because he so quickly turns his gaze from his own truth-seeking motives to those of others, he manages to avoid the awkward issue of how he can claim to love the truth while acknowledging that he has no real desire to *search* for it.

In this section, I have sought to tell a story about the vicar's truth-seeking motives which is more problematic than the standard interpretation of *The Profession* suggests. We have seen that the vicar, having begun his account by assuring the audience of his sincerity and profound love of truth, goes on to systematically undermine these assurances both by disingenuously defending behavior that is manifestly irresponsible and by ignoring the very real possibility that his inquiry could be biased by the influence of epistemically irrelevant desires. At this point, then, we have good reason to think that the vicar's moral and religious beliefs are motivated largely by nontruth-related interests. In the next section, I shall build on this basis by showing that the vicar's is not merely a case of motivated belief but rather of *self-deception*: he not only holds questionable or dubious beliefs but seems to do so knowingly, deploying a variety of epistemically irresponsible practices (e.g., rationalization, "whataboutism," denial, selective attention and perception, and so on) to defend them.

The Epistemology of Sincerity: The Belief-Adoption Process

So far I have sought to illustrate the ways in which the vicar's epistemically irrelevant desires compromise his attempt to discover the truth about "things that are important for us to know" (*E*, 268). Now I shall seek to show that *The Profession* does not depict a case of mere motivated belief but rather one of *self-deception*. I have already provided some preliminary evidence on this score by showing how the vicar's attempt at self-exculpation exhibits certain characteristics which we associate with self-deceptive belief, but I want to reinforce this case by examining his conception of the belief-adoption process. In *The Profession*, the vicar shows an interest not only in what beliefs increase happiness and reduce anxiety but also in how we can facilitate the formation of those beliefs.

The vicar's fundamental stratagem in this regard is epistemological. He seeks to understand how he comes into the possession of knowledge and then to use that information as a way of reinforcing his preferred version of reality. This objective is especially evident in his analysis of the relationship between sensation and judgment. Sensation, for the vicar, is the foundation of all knowledge. Without it we could know neither ourselves nor the world: "my sensations take place in me since they make me sense my existence; but their cause is external to me, since they affect me without my having anything to do with it. Thus not only do I exist, but there exist other beings—the objects of my sensations" (*E*, 270). Note that it is the *passivity* of sensation that gives us reliable access to the external world: we can, that is, reasonably trust in the accuracy of our sensations precisely because we have "*nothing* to do with producing or annihilating" them. Because sensation affects us irrespective of our wishes, our experience of them should be less conditioned by prior beliefs, biases, and other motivational distortions than are other cognitive functions (e.g., our judgments—see below). Thus however much our experience with the world beyond the self may be mediated and uncertain, the vicar nonetheless affirms that our organs of sense can, due to their passivity, be broadly trusted to give us access to physical objects "such as they are in nature." His belief in the passivity, and hence the reliability, of our raw physical sensations helps explain why he disregards so many of the issues central to early modern epistemology. He is untroubled by Descartes's evil demon, the precise nature of mental representation, or more generally by what is now called the problem of the external world. Because he can find no solid reason to question the existence of a mind-independent reality, he decides not to do so: "all the disputes of idealists and materialists signify nothing to me. Their distinctions…are chimeras" (*E*, 270).

Unfortunately, however, the very passivity which makes sensation reliable also limits its epistemic utility. Our individual perceptions may be reliable representations of the external world but the vicar notes that they are meaningless until they are integrated by the intelligent, thinking subject into a coherent and continuous flow of experience. A being abandoned solely to the slices of information provided by his senses would on the vicar's view have a highly fragmented sense of reality because he would be unable to grasp the relations which link the objects of consciousness together: "if we were purely passive in the use of our senses, there would be no communication among them. It would be impossible for us to know that the body we touch and the object we see are the same" (*E*, 271). Sensations are "separated" and "isolated" slices of information that must be compared, assessed, and synthesized to acquire genuine truth value. In this sense they are akin to points on a trend line, which represent particular observations with perfect accuracy but fail to disclose the *meaning* of the line as a whole.

Because disconnected bits of raw sense data do not announce their own meaning, some extra-sensory faculty is required to give them continuity and significance. The vicar assigns this crucial function to the capacity for *judgment*, which makes knowledge of the physical world possible by allowing us to discover the relations which connect our otherwise isolated sensations: "to perceive is to sense; to compare is to judge. Judging and sensing are not the same thing. By sensation, objects are presented to me separated, isolated, such as they are in nature. By comparison I move them, I transport them.... I superimpose them on one another in order to pronounce on their difference or their likeness" (*E*, 270). Our ability to judge not only enables a fully integrated experience of the world by allowing our sensory systems to talk to each other but also gives us the ability to identify systematic patterns and draw inferences from them. Thus for the vicar, it is judgment and not sensation that makes knowledge acquisition possible and raises us to the level of "intelligent" beings: "Therefore, I am not simply a sensitive and passive being but an active and intelligent being; and whatever philosophy may say about it, I shall dare to pretend to the honor of thinking" (*E*, 272). Judgment, then, is distinct from sensation in that it is "active" where the latter is "passive:" it is directed purposively by the "intelligent" subject rather than reflexively and unthinkingly absorbed by him.

Though the capacity to analyze one's sensations makes knowledge possible, it also introduces the problem of *error* along with that possibility. Indeed, it is precisely because the subject actively directs the process of "comparing" his various sensations that it is so unpredictable and mistake-prone: "I know only that the truth is in things and not in the mind which judges them, and that the less of myself I put into the judgments I make, the more sure I am of approaching the truth" (*E*, 272). The vicar here claims that contingent human judgment is the source of our most significant errors and that we are simply too weak, too fallible, and too susceptible to our passions to place much trust in our rational faculties (*E*, 268). Thus it would seem that the very capacity which puts truth within our grasp also moves it further away, and the vicar—having invoked the faculty of judgment to escape the flux of a purely sensory existence—now must confront the chaos introduced by his own intelligent subjectivity.

In his quest for truth, then, the vicar has encountered a serious problem. He has discovered both that his sensory faculties are reliable but insufficient for knowledge and that the capacity for judgment—which makes knowledge possible—is deeply unreliable. His proposed resolution to this problem, as evidenced by the passage above, is to ensure that his judgments flow as immediately from his sensations as possible. This approach would, in principle, allow him to combine the brute accuracy of raw sensation with the range, creativity, and reflective intelligence of judgment and give him a basis for believing that the order he perceives in the universe is not an artifact of his imagination but is rather a genuine part of the thing itself.

Unfortunately, however, the vicar does not ground his judgments about Nature upon a reliable basis of sensation as he pledges to do. To the contrary, he lets his subjective judgments govern his patterns of perception so that he takes notice of only those aspects of the natural world which are compatible with his preferred interpretation of it. In this vein, the vicar himself quietly revises his initial claims about the passivity of sensation, observing that human beings do not give equal attention to the phenomena which surround them but instead perceive the world in a selective, discriminating way: "Let this or that name be given to this force in my mind which brings together and compares my sensations....It is still true that it is in me and not in things, although I produce it only on the occasion of the impression made on me by objects. *Without being master of sensing or not sensing, I am the master of giving more or less examination to what I sense*" (*E*, 273, emphasis added). The vicar notes here that our sensations are actually *not* purely passive but are instead permeated with and structured by a variety of implicit judgments about what is and is not worthy of notice: while it is perhaps not in our power to notice or not notice a physical object, it *is* in our power to determine how much and what kind of attention that object merits. Possessing this power allows us to attune ourselves to reality in a selective and intelligent way, focusing our conscious attention where it is needed and letting the less salient features of our experience recede into the background.

It is not difficult to see how the ability to focus one's attention in discriminating ways could serve to reinforce one's preexisting beliefs without our realizing that this is happening—indeed, Rousseau himself notes the ways in which his "automatic impulses" tracked his interests and desires without any guidance from consciousness (*R*, 49)—but the vicar claims to be "the master" of this process and expresses a desire to subject it to conscious control and direction. Given his emphasis on his sincere love of truth, one might assume that he would want to become aware of the implicit judgments structuring his sensory activity so that he could identify and eliminate any subjective biases that may have subconsciously crept into his thinking, but far from wanting to get rid of such biases he instead wants to *reinforce* them. His desire in this regard is most conspicuous in his effort to demonstrate his first article of faith, namely that "a will moves the universe and animates nature" (*E*, 273). This claim is based on the straightforward, if questionable, assumption that "scattered and dead" matter cannot move itself and thus owes its motion to a first mover. But it is noteworthy less for its content than for the way in which it is justified:

> This same universe is in motion; and in its motion, which is regular, uniform, and subjected to constant laws, it contains nothing of that liberty appearing in the spontaneous motions of man and the animals.... Therefore there is some cause of its motions external to it, *one which I do not perceive*. But inner persuasion makes this cause so evident to my senses that I cannot see the sun rotate *without imagining* a force that pushes it; or if the earth turns, *I believe I sense* a hand that makes it turn. (*E*, 273, emphasis added)

Though the vicar initially claims that his judgments about the world will be reliable only to the degree that they are founded on his sensations, he now acknowledges here that he "do[es] not perceive" the ultimate cause of motion and that his belief in God-as-prime-mover is founded on extra-sensory intuition—"inner persuasion"—rather than on anything related to his sensations. On this point, he notes that he cannot observe a celestial body's movement without simultaneously *imagining* "a force that pushes it" and, still more revealingly, that when he sees the earth turn, he *believes he senses* (as opposed to merely sensing) "a hand that makes it turn." The vicar's phraseology gives the lie to his claim to follow Nature in his quest to understand the world and reveals that, having promised to derive his beliefs about the world from his sensations, he instead allows his beliefs to structure his patterns of perception.

It is very odd that the vicar articulates a complex and highly interesting theory of belief-formation only to ignore it when it comes to belief-*adoption*. Indeed, one wonders why he goes to the trouble of explaining in precise detail how a sincere belief in intelligent design might form only to disregard that very explanation in describing the genesis of his own beliefs. But appealing to self-deception helps resolve this puzzle, for it uncovers the possibility that the vicar's epistemological argument was never intended to attain truth in the first place: what his conflation of sense perception and judgment actually allows him to do is to confer an unwarranted feeling of certainty upon the complex, contestable inferences he makes about the character of the universe while giving his beliefs a veneer of plausibility. It is the interest in mitigating anxiety, rather than anything truth-related, that directs the vicar's inquiry. Thus we are left with the suspicion that the feeling of sincerity which is supposed to direct his inquiry is instead the product of it, and that the point of his entire enterprise is not to search for the truth in good faith so much as to identify a means by which he can come to believe sincerely in that which he does not sincerely believe.

Conclusion

In this essay I have argued that the Savoyard Vicar of Rousseau's *Emile*—almost always viewed as an exemplar of sincerity and often identified as a mouthpiece for Rousseau himself—is not only not sincere in his quest for truth but is also guilty of self-deception. I have made this argument by (1) showing that the vicar's inquiry is motivated and influenced throughout by the nontruth-related interests he has in preserving his self-esteem and mitigating his anxiety, and (2) revealing the epistemological program which allows him to confer a feeling of certainty upon beliefs that he himself knows are not fully justified. In making this case I have emphasized the willful and perhaps even fully intentional character of the vicar's errors and, in so doing, have shown how they are distinct from, and more serious than, garden variety motivated believing and other, more minor, forms of epistemic failure.

To the degree that the vicar's errors can be said to be willful or deliberate, important questions remain about exactly how he manages to avoid awareness of them. Such avoidance would seem to be necessary to the effective execution of a self-deceptive program, for if one is fully aware that a belief he holds is based on faulty reasoning or flawed evidence then it is difficult to understand how he can steadfastly and sincerely hold that belief. Thus what a successful self-deceiver needs is some means of concealing his errors from himself, some way of keeping his own lingering reservations at the margins of consciousness. We have already seen that the vicar employs selective attention as a means to this end, constantly shifting his focus in ways that allow him to reinforce his preferred interpretation of reality and prevent him from having to engage directly with the problems with his view, but I would like to close by suggesting that the vicar employs another self-deceptive stratagem worthy of note—he deceives himself about his own truthfulness.[20] On this point, we have already noted the extent to which the vicar's conception of truth-telling depends on the premise of his sincerity: he consistently invokes his good faith and sincere love of truth as a reason to trust him and to take his account of truth-seeking seriously (if not to accept it outright). He, then, is clearly persuaded of his own inner-sincerity and believes himself to be a certain kind of person, namely a *truthful* one.

---

[20] Matt Sleat, "Self-Deception about Truthfulness," *European Journal of Philosophy* 30, no. 2 (June 2022): 693–708.

Now, given the substantial evidence that the vicar has overestimated—perhaps drastically—his commitment to truthfulness, we must wonder what factors might have led him to misunderstand himself in this way and what psychological functions such a misunderstanding might serve. On these scores, it should first be noted that there is nothing all that odd about the fact that the vicar exaggerates his sincerity—self-enhancement bias is a normal and predictable human tendency which we should not be surprised to find the vicar exemplifying, especially given (1) his explicitly stated need to preserve his self-esteem, and (2) how dependent his self-esteem is on maintaining a belief in his own truthfulness. The (false) belief in his own sincerity also appears to serve a further, related function: when the vicar ascribes to himself the *character trait* of truthfulness this leads him to make the default assumption that his beliefs are developed and maintained in good faith. Once, that is, the vicar is assured of his own sincerity he begins interpreting his own doxastic activity through that lens and assigning the quality of truthfulness to everything he feels and believes: "I only have to consult myself about what I want to do," he tells the boy as he articulates his conception of conscience. "*Everything I sense to be good is good; everything I sense to be bad is bad.* The best of all casuists is conscience" (*E*, 286, emphasis added). To the degree that the vicar's feelings and beliefs are definitionally sincere—they are sincere *because* he believes them—it becomes a relatively easy matter for him to swat away concerns about his own good faith and intellectual honesty: he can simply reject such concerns as being inconsistent with his character. It is, I suspect, in this way that the vicar manages to evade or at least mitigate the everyday anxieties that attend self-deception and to maintain some degree of psychological serenity even while being in some way aware of the problems associated with his beliefs.

If the vicar can indeed be said to be engaged in self-deception, we may still wonder about the ultimate significance of this claim. Does the imputation of a self-deceptive intention serve to undermine the vicar's status as a moral (and political) exemplar? Without denying that the interpretation I have developed is subversive in important respects, I also wish to emphasize that the vicar would hardly be the only self-deceiver among Rousseau's exemplars. Thus it is hardly a question of whether the vicar is exemplary so much as a question of what, exactly, he exemplifies. On this score, consider that Rousseau himself repeatedly emphasizes not only that religious beliefs need not be true in order to be *useful* and that many useful beliefs may well be false:

> I therefore see two ways to examine and compare the various religions. One is according to what is true and false in them....The other is according to their temporal and moral effects on earth, according to the good or evil they can do for society and the human race. *One must not begin...by deciding that these two things always go together, and that the truest religion is also the most social. That is precisely what is in question.*"[21]

Rousseau's distinction between truth and utility puts religious believers like the vicar in a difficult situation, for if religious beliefs are to serve the salutary psychological and social functions which Rousseau assigns to them then the believers themselves must think that their beliefs are not *merely* consoling or conducive to virtue but also that they are *true*.

---

[21] Jean-Jacques Rousseau, *Letter to Beaumont, Letters Written from the Mountain, and Related Writings* in *Collected Writings of Rousseau*, ed. Christopher Kelly and Eve Grace, trans. Christopher Kelly and Judith R. Bush (Hanover, NH: Dartmouth College Press, 2001), 9:54. Emphasis added.

6.

TRAVEL AS PHILOSOPHIC EDUCATION IN *EMILE*

Denise Schaeffer

On Travel is one of three sections of Rousseau's *Emile* that are marked off by their own subtitles: *The Profession of Faith of the Savoyard Vicar* in book four; the section of book five subtitled *Sophie, or the Woman*; and, also within book five, the section subtitled *On Travel (Des Voyages)*. Of the three, *On Travel* has received the least scholarly attention. This treatise-within-a-treatise can be further divided into two parts that are separated by an explicit transition. The first part poses the question of the value of travel and outlines some general principles for traveling well, whereas the second part purports to "unite" (*E*, 458)[1] the comparative study of governments with the study of the principles of political right, specifically with a view toward enabling Emile to select an ideal place of residence for his future family. As such, it is tempting to consider *On Travel* solely in the context of Emile's political or civic education.

The journey described in *On Travel*, however, is not the only journey that Emile and his tutor undertake in book five. As is the case for several other thematized lessons in Emile's education, there is a sort of prequel that may seem relatively insignificant on the surface but in fact plays an important role in setting up the

---

[1] *E*, cited by page, will refer to Jean-Jacques Rousseau, *Emile, or On Education*, ed. and trans. Allan Bloom (New York: Basic Books, 1979).

more explicit instruction.[2] In this case, when Emile reaches marriageable age, he and his tutor go to Paris, ostensibly to search for a wife. But Rousseau reveals to the reader that it is only a "feigned" search (*E*, 407), since he has already identified the perfect companion for Emile. The tutor equips Emile with an idealized image of a woman named Sophie and predicts that this internalized image of a future beloved will shape Emile's romantic inclinations and protect him from the temptations of the big city. Rousseau does not provide any narrative details about their journey to Paris or their fruitless search while there. Rather, he announces that he will present "a kind of essay on true taste in the choice of agreeable leisure" (*E*, 354). Their original purpose of searching for a wife is mentioned again only in passing as something they conducted "while passing the time" (*E*, 354). However, when it is time to leave, Rousseau devotes several pages to discussing the "method" that will govern their journey away from Paris to the countryside. Since the search for a wife was in fact (though unbeknownst to Emile) only a feigned search, the travel itself seems to have been the point. Rousseau's discussion of the "method" that governs the journey from Paris to Sophie's residence is his first thematization of travel in book five, and, as we shall see, the method that he presents bears little resemblance to the one he subsequently advocates in *On Travel.*

Twice, then, Rousseau steps outside of the dramatic narrative of book five to discuss travel thematically—first in the context of the journey from Paris to Sophie's family home, and again in the first part of the section formally subtitled *On Travel.* Throughout both discussions, Rousseau reinforces several points made earlier in *Emile* and elsewhere in his writings. Broadly

[2] For further discussion of this pattern in *Emile*, see Denise Schaeffer, *Rousseau on Education, Freedom and Judgment* (University Park: The Pennsylvania State University Press, 2014).

speaking, the two treatments of travel correspond to the two stages (negative and positive) in Emile's education (books 1–3 and 4–5, respectively), as I shall demonstrate below. The pronounced differences between the two discussions of travel invite us to consider whether and how they might form a coherent whole—a question mirrored in the structure of *Emile*. Notably, in both discussions, Rousseau refers to a "philosophic" way of traveling. Philosophy is a tacit but significant theme throughout book five insofar as Emile is being educated to become a lover not simply of Sophie but of *Sophia*.[3] Thus, a comprehensive analysis of the issue of travel in *Emile* should encompass both the first journey that the tutor and his pupil undertake together in book five as well as the section formally subtitled *On Travel*.[4] This analysis will reveal that travel functions as more than a plot device in the dramatic courtship of Emile and Sophie, and as more than a delivery mechanism for Emile's political education. Ultimately, Rousseau presents travel as the capstone to Emile's philosophic education.

Fleeing Paris, Pursuing Philosophy

The tutor's desired effect in equipping his pupil with an internalized image of ideal feminine virtue is borne out. Emile is disdainful as they leave Paris, viewing their search as a waste of time (*E*, 410). Rousseau explains to the reader that he and his pupil will embark on their journey "like true knights errant" (*E*, 410). He is

[3] See also Laurence D. Cooper, "*Emile*, or On Philosophy?" chap. 6 in *Eros in Plato, Rousseau, and Nietzsche: The Politics of Infinity* (University Park: The Pennsylvania State University Press, 2007).

[4] Gallēri similarly takes this approach of addressing both of book 5's sections on travel in tandem, though his theoretical concerns differ. See Gábor Gelléri, *Lessons of Travel in Eighteenth-Century France: From Grand Tour to School Trips* (Suffolk, UK: Boydell Press, 2020).

quick to clarify that by this he does not mean that they are seeking adventures—on the contrary, they "flee" adventures in leaving Paris behind. The resemblance is only in the pace of their travel, which will be languorous. In other words, Rousseau implies that the tutor and Emile are simultaneously fleeing (Paris) and moving slowly toward their destination. It is the slowness that Rousseau emphasizes in the general guidance about travel that immediately follows. Rousseau begins by reminding readers to attend to the "spirit" rather than the letter of his method. Those who do will not be surprised that he and his pupil will not travel in the typical manner, "asleep in a well-closed post-chaise, progressing without seeing or observing anything" (*E*, 410). Rather, they will travel by foot as much as possible. Rousseau then digresses on the subjective experience of time, articulating and countering the conventional view that "life is short" and that one should therefore be efficient in spending one's time. Such thoughtless pronouncements, in Rousseau's view, reflect a fundamental misunderstanding about the human relationship to time, and the value of the interval that separates individuals from their goals, which they are so impatient to achieve. His critique of this notion recalls the earliest phase of Emile's upbringing, during which Rousseau had strongly advised the reader not to rush childhood. There, he had described the method of his negative education as knowing how "to lose time in order to gain it" (*E*, 141). In that same spirit, he now rejects the pursuit of speed and efficiency in travel, which, by trying to save time, only wastes it.

Further developing this critique of the modern obsession with speed and goal achievement, Rousseau observes that most people rush from place to place, appreciating nothing along the way. Owing to this haste, they are unable to enjoy life. Even when they travel, they rush to their destination, only so that they can more quickly get back to work. In short, the typical person hurries simply in order to hurry. Emile, in contrast, has been raised to "enjoy life." He does not hurry; therefore he "is always more where he is than where he will be" (*E*, 411). This description calls to mind the natural man of book one, and the contrast between natural man and the bourgeois, who is always where he is not. Traveling by foot facilitates Emile's resemblance to natural man. However, natural man does not travel; he simply wanders. Rousseau now adds a tiny wrinkle, noting that Emile will travel by foot rather than by horse "unless he is in a hurry" (*E*, 411). He immediately poses a question: "but why would Emile ever be in a hurry?" One might expect this to be a purely rhetorical question requiring no response, but Rousseau explicitly answers his question by saying that it would be "for one reason alone—to enjoy life" (*E*, 411). In other words, Emile is in a hurry to enjoy life—an enjoyment that requires *not* being in a hurry. This paradoxical remark suggests that perhaps certain things that Rousseau criticizes as detrimental to human happiness and freedom, including haste, may potentially be redirected in the service of those very same ends.

In this spirit, Rousseau further elaborates the virtues of traveling by foot. Unlike traveling in a carriage, walking allows for direct sensory engagement with one's surroundings. Here we detect echoes of the middle stage of Emile's pre-adolescent education, specifically his scientific education about the physical world. Just as in book three Emile learned the scientific method by interacting directly with natural phenomena, here Rousseau describes how, when traveling on foot, one can pursue one's curiosity about the streams, rocks and trees one encounters along the way. One might recall a younger Emile asking, "Why did this stone fall?" (*E*, 177). Here, we are told that Emile will be able to encounter a variety of natural objects and phenomena in their natural state—in quarries and forests, not in museums, as those who travel to cities must do. Rousseau goes on to insist that one who travels in this way is at complete liberty, depending on no one. "I do not need to choose ready-made paths....I see all that a man can see, and depending only on myself, I enjoy all the liberty a man can enjoy" (*E*, 412). In keeping with such complete liberty, the journey is characterized as being entirely aimless, without a predetermined agenda or goal. "One object attracts us to another, and we always go forward" (*E*, 412). Proceeding willy-nilly, as impulse or inclination dictates, such a traveler will stop to examine whatever catches his interest, and the moment enjoyment ends or boredom strikes, he moves on. This gives the impression of being completely self-directed, a self-moved mover—that is, of one's movements having no cause outside of one's own inclinations.

This is an illusion, of course, since the tutor is guiding Emile ultimately to Sophie's family's home, but it is an illusion that Rousseau leverages to make a larger point. First, it subtly undermines the apparent binary contrast between goal-orientedness and aimlessness. Aiming at aimlessness turns aimlessness itself into a goal. The point is to be simultaneously mindful and forgetful of one's goal, rather than to pretend (as he does with Emile, though not the reader) that there is no goal. The tutor's deception also tacitly raises the problem of self-knowledge. While here he maintains that he and his pupil will simply follow their inclinations as they trek forward, Rousseau makes clear in various other writings that it is not so easy to know one's own inclinations and to be sure that they are truly one's own. In the Sixth Walk of the *Reveries of the Solitary Walker*, for example, Rousseau resolves to follow only his inclinations, but, despite his best effort, repeatedly finds his inclinations to be shaped by external factors, including other people's actions and expectations.[5] And yet the illusion of self-direction and claims of being at "complete liberty" persist throughout this brief account of the time spent between Paris and the pair's arrival at the country home of Sophie's family. Furthermore, the description is explicitly connected to philosophy. Extoling the virtues of this way of traveling, Rousseau states that "to travel on foot is to travel like Thales, Plato, and Pythagoras" (*E*, 412). What does he mean by this? On one level, the answer seems straightforward: direct engagement with the natural world, unmediated by books or any other sources of authority, is designed to prevent the development of prejudice so that Emile's mind can operate independently. Such independence of mind is a foundational quality of Emile's philosophic education.

Rousseau does not stop there, however. Following the reference to traveling like the ancient philosophers, Rousseau adds that he cannot imagine a more philosophic way to travel. Yet he *does* go on to imagine and discuss at length a starkly different mode of traveling in the upcoming section *On Travel*. There, Rousseau's discussion concerns a two-year voyage to several different countries, which of course cannot be completed on foot. Despite this difference, Rousseau again refers to Plato and Pythagoras as models. Since both discussions feature these philosopher figures, but are so very different, his remark poses an implicit question: *is* there another way of traveling that is philosophic—and perhaps even *more* philosophic than the method Rousseau initially utilizes with his pupil as they leave Paris behind? Taking Rousseau's question seriously, rather than simply as a rhetorical flourish, raises the possibility that *On Travel*, in addition to

[5] For an extended discussion of this point, see Michael Davis, *The Autobiography of Philosophy: Rousseau's* The Reveries of the Solitary Walker (Lanham, MD: Rowman & Littlefield, 1999), 189–209.

whatever else it may accomplish in the dramatic narrative of *Emile*, is in part an answer to this question.

Travel in *On Travel*

The explicitly stated reasons for sending Emile on a two-year journey are to test the fidelity of the two young lovers through an extended absence, as well as to enable Emile to choose the ideal locale for their future abode. However, Rousseau makes clear that there is a philosophical issue underlying the practical goal of finding the best place to live. Just as he prepares to announce this goal to his imagined pupil, Rousseau explains to the reader that he needs to "give the young man a palpable interest in informing himself" (*E*, 455). The practical objective is meant to motivate the pursuit of knowledge. In stark contrast to his earlier description of moving spontaneously from one spot to another, Rousseau now insists that travel should be goal oriented and that there must be formal rules if one wants to travel well. Indeed, he explicitly reverses the emphasis on journey versus destination, and contends that travelling for the sake of travelling, to "wander" without a goal, makes one a mere "vagabond" (*E*, 455). To be sure, the context for the travel has changed, but more fundamentally the shift implies that both aimless travel and goal-oriented travel can be done either poorly or well. And if genuine travel, as opposed to mere mobility, is marked by its purposefulness, the question becomes what the proper purpose(s) of travel ought to be. This question dominates Rousseau's general reflections in the first half of *On Travel*.

Rousseau begins the formally subtitled section by making reference to the standard question at the heart of Enlightenment-era debates[6] about the pedagogical value of travel: "it is asked whether it is good for young people to travel." Rousseau then puts the question "differently," proposing that one might ask instead "whether it is good that men have traveled" (*E*, 446). This reformulation does two things. Firstit shifts the emphasis from the experience itself to the result. Second, it shifts the emphasis from youth to people in general. This anticipates what will become the central issue in the first half of *On Travel.*

Having posed (and then revised) his initial question,[7] Rousseau launches into a critique of book learning that similarly underscores a tension between the prospective and the retrospective: "believing that we know what we have read, we believe that we can dispense with [further] learning" (*E*, 446). Turning his attention specifically to travelogues and the question of whether they can teach us about nations and peoples other than our own, Rousseau rejects books in favor of learning from "the book of the world." Drawing on a phrase used by Descartes,[8] Rousseau here engages with longstanding debates about pedagogical travel and the value of travelogues in particular.[9] He also recalls his own

[6] For an overview of these debates, see Gelléri, *Lessons of Travel in Eighteenth-Century France*; Nigel Leask, "Eighteenth Century Travel Writing" in *The Cambridge History of Travel Writing* (Cambridge: Cambridge University Press, 2019); and Jenny Mander, "Eighteenth-Century Travel," in *The Cambridge History of French Literature*, ed. William Burgwinkle, Nicholas Mammond and Emma Wilson (Cambridge: Cambridge University Press, 2011). As Gelléri explains, "In eighteenth-century France, while travelogues were widely read and enjoyed in practice...criticism of travel literature was omnipresent" (113).

[7] For a more detailed discussion of the significance of this reformulation, see Juliette Morice, "Voyage et anthropologie dans l'Émile de Rousseau," *Revue de métaphysique et de morale* 77, no. 1 (2013): 127–42.

[8] René Descartes, *Discourse on Method*, part 1.

[9] See, for example, Gelléri, "Travelling on a Moebius strip: Émile's travels," chap. 4 in *Lessons of Travel in Eighteenth-Century France*; and Georges

vehement rejection of all books (other than *Robinson Crusoe*) in book three of *Emile*. However, just as in book three Rousseau qualified his general rule with this one exception, in *On Travel* his apparently wholesale dismissal of the pedagogical value of travelogues in favor of "the book of the world" is more complex than may first appear.

Rousseau begins by positing an inverse proportion between the number of "histories and accounts of voyages" published in any nation and the prevalence of actual knowledge about "the genius and morals of other nations." The problem is twofold: "so great a number of books makes us neglect the book of the world; or if we still read in it, each sticks to his own page" (*E*, 451). In other words, the problem is not simply that reading books dissuades us from engaging directly with the world, but also that books tend to reinforce biases that continue to operate even when one is directly experiencing the world. Parisians, for example, believe they "know men" but in fact cannot make sense of a single foreign individual when they meet one. They have "read perhaps ten times the description of a country" and yet "one of its inhabitants will be an object of wonder" (*E*, 451). While it may appear that one's knowledge of human variability would expand by virtue of reading widely about other cultures, Rousseau contends that such reading fosters an overly generic perspective in which cultural differences are elided. As a result, when individual foreigners are encountered outside of these generic descriptions, they appear to be sui generis and are regarded "as an extraordinary phenomenon which has no equal in the rest of the universe" (*E*, 451). This problem is not averted by reading diverse accounts from multiple travelers who relay their individual experiences. As Rousseau explains, "I have spent my life reading accounts of

---

Van Pen Abbeele, "Pedestrian Rousseau," chap. 4 in *Travel as Metaphor: From Montaigne to Rousseau* (Minneapolis: University of Minnesota Press, 1992).

travel, and I have never found two which have given me the same idea of the same people" (*E*, 451). In other words, Rousseau simultaneously insists that generic accounts are too generic and that particular accounts are too particular.

Rousseau concludes from these difficulties that "one must not read, one must see." Having set up this binary contrast between reading books, on the one hand, and direct observation, on the other, he now devotes attention to the challenges of learning to see. He reformulates his guiding question yet again: "Hence there is another way of putting the same question about travel: does it suffice for a well-educated man to know only his compatriots, or is it important for him to know men in general?" (*E*, 451). Rousseau has introduced a new consideration—the question of *how*, as opposed to *whether*, to travel. And he concurrently provides the standard of judgment, which is that travel ought to be geared to knowing "men in general" (*les hommes en général*; *E*, 451). This phrase stands in opposition to his earlier refeèence to the goal of knowing "the genius and morals of other nations," which implied knowledge of a variety of particulars. The goal of knowing "men in general," in contrast, suggests that one must grasp the universal. With this, Rousseau shifts from an anthropological to a philosophical frame for his subsequent discussion of travel.

The value of knowing men in general as opposed to being familiar only with one's compatriots, is "no longer" in "either dispute or doubt." He concedes that we can take for granted that it is necessary to expose one's pupil to other peoples and cultures, as lack of such broadening exposure can leave one in a narrowly parochial state. "Whoever has seen only one people does not know men; he knows only the people with whom he has lived." But this raises a further question about method: "If one wants to know men, is it necessary to roam the entire earth?...Is it necessary to know all the individuals to know the species?" (*E*, 451). Rousseau's answer is an unqualified "No." Endless roaming is neither necessary nor sufficient. But if the desired general perspective does not automatically emerge from exposure to myriad particulars, nor from reading books, how then is it to be achieved?

> [I]t is not sufficient to roam through various countries. It is necessary to know how to travel. To observe, it is necessary to have eyes and to turn them toward the object one wants to know. There are many persons who are informed still less by travel than by books, because they are ignorant of the art of thinking; because when they read, their minds are at least guided by the author; and because when they travel, they do not know how to see anything on their own. (*E*, 452)

Developing the ability to see for oneself requires more than the absence of external interference. Books often get in the way of cultivating this ability, because "it is too much to have to pierce through both the authors' prejudices and our own" (*E*, 451), but at the same time a person does not spontaneously know how to "read" the text of the world. For some, an author's guidance may be beneficial, as they "do not know how to see anything on their own" (*E*, 452). Moreover, even when reading "the book of the world" a person might still stick only to "his own page," as mentioned earlier. (One thinks here of the student who "studies abroad" but chooses to spend time only with fellow travelers, not with locals.) Rousseau, a vigorous defender of what today we call "experiential learning," was profoundly aware that one can experience something and still not *experience* it, much less learn from it.

Even as Rousseau explores the question of how one learns to see the truth of "men in general" he simultaneously emphasizes the difficulty of truly seeing the particulars. One problem is the vanishing distinctiveness of particular places and peoples in an increasingly homogenized world. Commerce, transportation, communication—all of these increase contact among nations and thereby facilitate the disappearance of "those national differences which previously struck the observer at first glance" (*E*, 453). Echoing the comparison of human nature to the statue of Glaucus in the Preface to the *Second Discourse*, he explains that "as the original character of a people fades from day to day, it becomes proportionately more difficult to grasp" (*E*, 453). To that end, he makes a very typical move (for Rousseau) which is to say that one should avoid the big capital cities, which resemble one another in their bland cosmopolitanism, and focus instead on the provinces, which preserve their distinctiveness. Paris and London strike Rousseau as practically the same city; "I know in advance how people live there." It is only in the remote provinces that "a people reveals its character and shows itself without admixture" (*E*, 468).

However, Rousseau does not advise skipping the capital cities altogether, as one might expect from the force of his critique. Instead, he remarks that one should visit the capital in passing before heading to the countryside. This suggests there is something to be learned from such cities, though it is certainly not the distinctive national character. But this lack of distinctiveness can itself be instructive. It is important to notice *that* inhabitants of cosmopolitan cities tend to be very similar, and that their national distinctions are blurred or even erased. It is against this backdrop of apparent similarity that the fading quality of distinct differences becomes visible and takes on significance. Rousseau wants the genuinely philosophic traveler to observe this tendency toward sameness without being taken in by it or assuming it to constitute the complete truth about men in general.

For a similar reason, even as Rousseau insists that untraveled people in the remote provinces reveal a nation's true character, he simultaneously indicates that one learns a lot about a nation's character from observing those of its citizenry who *do* travel—that is, from *how* they travel. He devotes an entire paragraph to comparing how the French travel and how the English travel, for example (*E*, 452). The critical difference, he explains, is seen in the different prejudices that they bring to their travel. Those prejudices, too, reveal something of the character of a particular nation's people. Thus, while one's own prejudices present an obstacle to truly "seeing" other human beings and reading the book of the world, prejudices in general are part of that book and can be instructive, if studied rather than simply absorbed. It is therefore not enough to observe only people who travel least. Seeing how people travel reveals dimensions of their particularity as much as observing them in an isolated context. Ultimately, Rousseau suggests that to know a people, one must observe them both in motion and at rest—traveling, and not traveling.

This leads him to return to the matter of books, as he affirms the value of preserving the wisdom of the ancients with regard to the distinct character of different peoples. Precisely because "they traveled little, read little and wrote few books" (*E*, 452), one finds in their books observations that are useful to the learning he seeks to foster in his pupil. Rousseau thus suggests that reading and traveling might, when done well and in limited amounts, serve the goals that they more typically tend to undermine. In fact, he concludes this part of his discussion by asking: "If we could...consider all the men who had ever lived, can it be doubted that we would find that they varied more from age to age than they do today from nation to nation?" (*E*, 454). What is at issue is the ability to discern genuine as opposed to superficial differences. The variation that becomes apparent through the survey of particulars can be organized and interpreted in more than one way. Learning to see is in part learning to see that the variability itself may vary—and to be able to discern which differences truly matter. The goal is not simply to observe the multiplicity but to raise questions of meaning and value. Ultimately, this is the most fundamental reason why "to roam the earth" is not the proper method for traveling.

Beyond the difficulty of discerning the faded particularities of distinct cultures, the other major obstacle that Rousseau discusses has to do with the aims that govern any program of travel. "The instruction one extracts from travel is related to the aim that causes travel to be undertaken" (*E*, 454). He identifies two aims that tend to impede the genuine learning that can come from travel. The first is commerce. When the "aim is profit, it absorbs all the attention of those who devote themselves to it" (*E*, 454). While commerce may bring people into contact with other cultures, it discourages genuine curiosity or engagement. "When they know the profit they can make from one another, what more do they have to know?" The second problematic aim is, somewhat surprisingly, associated with philosophy. When the aim is "a system of philosophy, the traveler never sees anything but what he wants to see" (*E*, 454). It is not philosophy itself that impedes genuine seeing; rather, it is the search for a philosophic system. The target of Rousseau's critique here is a particular type of philosophy. Indeed, he goes on to assert that sometimes even those who appear to travel with non-commercial intentions, are, it turns out, interested in profit. "It is said that we have learned men who travel to inform themselves. This is an error. The learned travel for profit like the others" (*E*, 454). The problem is that they often travel at the behest and expense of the court, which in turn determines their aims. Even as he concedes that there are a few learned men who travel at their own expense, Rousseau demurs that "it is never to study men but rather to instruct them." Such travelers seek "not science" but "ostentation." Overall, he concludes, most people—even those who claim to seek knowledge—travel "for the sake of opinion." And because they travel for the sake of opinion, they are unlikely to "learn to shake off the yoke of opinion in their travels" (*E*, 454).

Is it any wonder, then, that Rousseau laments that "the Platos and the Pythagorases are no longer to be found" (*E*, 454). While critiquing the false philosophers (i.e., those motivated by ostentation and opinion) who populate the modern world, Rousseau invokes these ancient figures to exemplify the philosophic perspective that he seeks to develop in his pupil. How should the goal of such travel be conceptualized? Even traveling with the goal of "inform[ing] oneself" is insufficient for Rousseau, for it is still "too vague an aim" (*E*, 455). He distinguishes between the merely "curious" and "someone who wants to philosophize" (*E*, 454). How, then, does Rousseau understand a genuinely philosophic approach to travel?

Travel as Education Toward Political Philosophy

When Emile is finally asked to choose where he would like to settle with Sophie, he announces that it makes no difference to him where he lives, since all existing political orders are flawed. "Give me Sophie and my field—and I shall be rich," he declares (*E*, 457). One might conclude that Emile has achieved the perspective that was the aim of his education in comparative government and the principles of political right. Those principles provided him with an understanding of what a legitimate and good political order should look like, and thus a standard against which to judge existing political orders as he surveys them throughout his travels. Against this standard, of course, we should expect him to find actually existing, particular governments wanting, and should not be surprised that he wishes to maintain his independence from all of them. This is, in part, a justifiable conclusion, insofar as independence is indeed a desired outcome of Emile's education. But it is only a part. The tutor's response is critical: "A field which is yours, dear Emile! And in what place will you choose it?" (*E*, 457). There is no field that is not somewhere in particular. Even the ongoing search for wisdom requires a particular home, insofar as the philosopher is an embodied human being. If Emile is in search of an abstract, universal field, he has misunderstood philosophy as well as citizenship.

The tutor later reproaches Emile for his "extravagant disinterestedness:"

> If I were speaking to you of the duties of the citizen, you would perhaps ask me where the fatherland is, and you would believe you had confounded me. But you would be mistaken, dear Emile, for he who does not have a fatherland at least has a country....Do not ask then, 'What difference does it make to me where I am?' It makes a difference to you that you are where you can fulfill all your duties, and one of those duties is an attachment to the place of your birth. Your compatriots protected you as a child; you ought to love them as a man. (*E*, 473–74)

Even as the tutor concedes that the true social contract is nowhere instantiated and observed, he insists that Emile must recognize some obligation to some particular set of laws of a particular place. He must choose his field somewhere in particular, and this is not a matter of indifference. To be sure, Rousseau does not want Emile to be taken in by the false appearances that surround him; at the same time, however, he does not want Emile to despise humanity in all of its deformity because he is attached only to an abstract ideal. Emile is surrounded by governments that are not truly legitimate fatherlands. But while this is a reality, so too is the fundamental reality of our essential human freedom.

To see men in general is to possess the ability to see both the real and the ideal at once: men as they are, *and* the essence of who they truly are apart from the corruption of modern social forces. This doubleness is reflected in *On Travel* insofar as Rousseau suggests that learning to see "men in general" requires a perspective that does not simply abstract from the particulars, nor simply encompasses them, but somehow achieves both at once.

This echoes the perspective that the tutor sought to inculcate in earlier stages of Emile's education as well. In the context of Emile's education in pity in book four, Rousseau advised that one must observe the spectacle of human folly from the proper distance. Observe "too closely" and the pupil will see "nothing from the good side," and soon "the general perversity will serve him less as a lesson than as an example" (*E*, 237). This carefully calculated middle distance is necessary in order to discern the doubleness that characterizes human beings who are both naturally good *and* corrupted. Rousseau desires that Emile "see that all men wear pretty much the same mask" but also "that there are faces more beautiful than the mask covering them" (*E*, 237). To see human beings as they really are is to see both of these things at once. Travel thus completes Emile's education in seeing "men in general," which encompasses a double view of them as both corrupted and good (i.e., more beautiful than the masks they wear). The parallel to Emile's political education might be stated in the following terms: let him see that all governments are deformed, but let him also know that there is an idea of government that is more beautiful than that. If *no* existing political orders are legitimate, Emile is likely to condemn every example he encounters. This does not facilitate his ability to choose a place to live, as he would be led to dismiss every possibility out of indifference. This, too, risks turning Emile into a "wanderer" who is at home everywhere but nowhere in particular and feels no responsibility toward anyone other than his own family. Such radical "wandering" entails a complete rejection of any sense of citizenship whatsoever. It turns one fully away from the political realm. But Emile is not a natural man, and the tutor reminds him that "he who has no fatherland at least has a country," to which he owes something (*E*, 473). As we have seen, Rousseau's aim is to achieve a certain doubleness that keeps the ideal in view but also exists in relationship to the flawed particular.

This double perspective is also reflected in the ultimate purpose of Emile's pedagogical journey, which requires him to both separate and connect the two senses of the term that describes the object of his love: Sophie and *Sophia*. Emile must learn to take his eyes off of the particular woman he loves in order to pursue wisdom. The tutor inculcates a set of ideal principles of political right and urges his pupil to set his eyes only on "imperishable beauty" (*E*, 446). At the same time, he teaches Emile that Sophie is not imperishable—some day she will die, and he must learn to bear her absence. The idea and the concrete particular must not be conflated, however, both must be kept in view. The exclusive fixation on either Sophie or *Sophia* might incline one toward the extravagant indifference that the tutor corrects in Emile by directing him back toward the human realm of particulars, even as he encourages his pupil to view those particulars always in light of an abstract ideal. The challenge of developing a stance that both is and is not embedded in a particular homeland (with all of its inevitable flaws) has a parallel in the treatment of philosophy that emerges through the complex discussion of travel, in which Rousseau explores the question of what it means to travel philosophically in part by distinguishing between positive and negative senses of what it means to wander. Emile's attachment to Sophie can function as a catalyst toward philosophy, as it motivates him to pursue the beautiful as well as knowledge of "men in general." However, if this pursuit leads him to value *only* that which can be abstracted from particular peoples and places, he might remain a wanderer in the negative sense criticized by Rousseau, rather than in the positive, more complex sense that he encourages over the course of his composite thematization of travel.

Emile is not meant to be a philosopher only in the sense evoked in the journey away from Paris—a philosopher gazing at the trees and stars (or even imperishable beauty) but ignorant of the human things and, especially, of himself. Nor is he meant to remain an unphilosophic wanderer, knowledgeable about particular governments but ignorant of the truth of "men in general" and the ideal "eternal laws" which cannot be found in any existing government (*E*, 473). Rather, Rousseau's answer to his own question about the most "philosophic" way of traveling requires a double vision that encompasses both the ideal and the particulars—and thus points us toward political philosophy.[10] Over the course of his composite thematization of travel, Rousseau twice evokes the examples of the ancient philosophers, which might appear to suggest a single, unified model. Ultimately, however, the argument about how to travel philosophically that develops over the course of book five shifts to affirm a model associated with Plato rather than with Thales, whose reputation for falling into a well while gazing up at the stars is well known. Perhaps this is why Thales drops out of Rousseau's second reference to the ancients. In the *Phaedo*, Plato's Socrates recounts his own intellectual turn—more precisely, his "flight"—from studying the natural sciences toward studying the *logoi*. This transformation,

[10] This is Rousseau's aspiration for his reader, at least, who is made privy to his thematic reflections on travel, even as his imaginary pupil is not. Whether Emile achieves this perspective or not is a question that would take us well beyond the subject of this essay.

described as a second sailing,[11] marks the beginning of Socrates's concern with examining questions that have ethical implications for how human beings live. In Rousseau's *Emile*, *On Travel* incorporates a similar "second sailing" regarding what it means to philosophize.

[11] Plato, *Phaedo*, lines 96–101.

7.

MISUNDERSTANDING ROUSSEAU: THE ENIGMAS OF *ROUSSEAU: JUDGE OF JEAN-JACQUES*

Christopher Kelly

Given Rousseau's fame both during his life and now, one would think that the last work that he completed would be an object of great attention. Indeed, both the *Confessions* and the *Reveries* were eagerly read when they appeared in the decade after his death even though both are incomplete. These two works were quickly recognized as masterpieces of French literature even in their unfinished state. His *Considerations on the Government of Poland* (completed in 1772) was also fairly quickly published, both in his collected writings and a separate edition. There were, however, two significant works that were published along with these that did not attract the same attention. These works continued to appear in editions of Rousseau's collected writings but were not published in separate editions until well into the twentieth century. There is no evidence that many people read them in the first hundred and fifty years they were available. The first of these is the *Essay on the Origin of Languages*. After a long period of neglect by all but a few scholars, this work was brought to attention by Jacques Derrida's *De la Grammatologie* in 1967. Since then, it has been studied just about as much as any of Rousseau's works. The other work is *Rousseau: Judge of Jean-Jacques:*

Dialogues (1772–1776).[1] This is, in fact, the last work that Rousseau completed. One reason for the relative lack of attention paid to it is that it is very peculiar, to such a degree that it is most often cited as evidence of Rousseau's insanity. It did not appear in an edition by itself until 1962, when it was published along with an introduction by Michel Foucault which gave it some attention, but only now, more than sixty years later, is it truly emerging from obscurity.

The work's strangeness appears in a simple description. It consists of three dialogues between two characters. One of them is named "Rousseau," but he is not exactly Jean-Jacques Rousseau, the author of this work and others. Rather, he is Rousseau as he would have been if he read the works rather than wrote them. The other character is identified simply as a Frenchman. In the First Dialogue he has not read the works because he has been persuaded that their author, called simply "Jean-Jacques," is a wicked criminal. In short, the three dialogues are concerned with the relationship between the books and the reputation of their author. The strangeness of the work reaches its peak when the character "Rousseau" gives an account of meeting "Jean-Jacques" and discovering that he is writing a book indistinguishable from the one we are reading: a character who is hard to distinguish from the author meets another such character in the act

---

[1] References to this work are from *Rousseau Judge of Jean Jacques: Dialogues* in Jean-Jacques Rousseau, *The Collected Writings of Rousseau*, ed. Roger D. Masters and Christopher Kelly, vol. 1 (Hanover, NH: University Press of New England, 1990–2010). This edition will be cited as *CW*. I have also consulted the best French edition: *Rousseau: Judge de Jean Jacques* (manuscript "Condillac") avec les variants ultérieures, ed. Jean-François Perrin, which is Tome XVIII in Jean-Jacques Rousseau, *Œuvres completes*, sous la direction de Jacques Bechtold, François Jacob, Christophe Martin et Yannick Séite (Paris: Classiques Garnier, 2016). Perrin has included many helpful notes to which I am indebted.

of creating both of them! I will argue that this strange work sheds important light on the issue of the public defense of a way of life that seems inexplicable to most people. In this latter respect, it can best be compared to Plato's *Apology of Socrates*.

I begin with the fact that readers have not found *Rousseau: Judge of Jean-Jacques* easy to understand. This is all the more interesting because its most overt theme is rampant misunderstandings about both "Jean-Jacques's" books and himself. In short, it has proven to be especially difficult to understand what Rousseau has to say about misunderstanding. His concern with this issue did not begin with *Rousseau: Judge of Jean-Jacques*. The continuity of this late work with earlier ones can be seen in his choice of its epigraph. In some, but not all, of the manuscripts, Rousseau begins with the Latin quotation, "Here I am the barbarian because no one understands me." This is a variant of a line from the Roman poet, Ovid, who writes about his exile to a barbarian land where the inhabitants do not understand Latin. Ovid is a sophisticated poet who lives far from his audience among people incapable of becoming his audience. This is a passage that had drawn Rousseau's attention long before he used it as the epigraph to *Rousseau: Judge of Jean-Jacques*.

The first occasion that we know of Rousseau using it occurred in 1742 when the twenty-nine-year-old Rousseau, who was living a provincial existence, wrote to a friend about his reading of philosophic and poetic literature, Leibniz and Pope in particular. After a lengthy discussion demonstrating his learning and intelligence, Rousseau concludes, "I hope, Sir, that in taking my frankness in the sense in which I offer it to you, it will have nothing that displeases you, and that you will pardon it in a man who speaks from experience, and who has numerous times had the occasion to say like Ovid among the Sarmathians. *Barbarbarus hic ego sum, quia non intelligor illis.*"[2] In other words, Rousseau identifies himself with the poet who lives among people too unsophisticated to understand him. Not long after this, he used the same remark from Ovid as the epigraph to a collection of short works that he published locally. Shortly after publishing this collection, Rousseau made his way to Paris where he hoped to achieve fame from a more sophisticated and, he hoped, receptive audience. The young man or woman from the provinces who longs for the cosmopolitan city where they will be understood and appreciated is a common theme in literature and life, explored by many writers other than Rousseau.

This repeated use of Ovid might seem to make unsurprising Rousseau's use of it once again in the work that finally made him famous, the *Discourse on the Sciences and the Arts* in 1751. There is, however, an entirely new element in Rousseau's use of this quotation as his epigraph. He has now been living among the sophisticated Parisians, with a short period in sophisticated and cosmopolitan Venice. It is no longer unsophisticated people from the provinces who mistakenly see Rousseau as even more barbaric than they are; it is now the learned and sophisticated readers of Paris and the academies of France whom Rousseau accuses (by anticipation) of misunderstanding. In effect, he predicts that his criticism of the sciences and arts will mistakenly be understood as coming from an ignorant barbarian rather than from a profound and intelligent analysis.

In fact, an essential part of the argument of the *Discourse* is that societies characterized by the promotion of the sciences and the arts fail to understand themselves. Rousseau first puts the issue in terms of what "an Inhabitant of some faraway land" would think about European morals on the basis of external

---

[2] *Correspondance complète de Jean Jacques Rousseau*, edited by R. A. Leigh (Oxford: Voltaire Foundation, 1965–1998), 1:139.

appearances. He says that such a foreigner, "would guess our morals to be exactly the opposite of what they are" (*FD*, *CW*, 2:7).[3] Here the issue seems to be the ability of the Europeans to deceive others, but Rousseau's analysis makes it clear that the Europeans also tend to think of themselves as morally superior to others because of their learning and mastery of the arts. As Rousseau says in a second epigraph, also from a Roman poet, Horace, "We are deceived by the appearance of right" (*FD*, *CW*, 2:4). What the sciences and the arts do is to spread a deceiving appearance that fools both outsiders and insiders. Even when sophisticated people see through these false appearances to a degree, they continue to congratulate themselves for their moral superiority over the less sophisticated. Rousseau's use of Ovid in this context, then, indicates that his audience, living in the impression that the sciences and arts support morality, will fail to understand his argument for the opposite position. In fact, this very misunderstanding is evidence of the truth of his position. By using the same epigraph twenty-five years later in the last work he completed, Rousseau indicates the continuing importance of the theme of misunderstanding for his work.

Rousseau certainly found that his prediction of misunderstanding applied to the critics who chose to attack the *First Discourse*. He said of one attack, "it is apparent on every page of the refutation that the Author does not understand or does not want to understand the work he refutes, which is assuredly very convenient for him," and adds, "no one has ever heard it said that a Painter who exhibits a work in public is obliged to examine the eyes of the spectators and furnish glasses for all of those who need

---

[3] *FD* refers to the *First Discourse*, or *Discourse on the Sciences and the Arts* in Jean-Jacques Rousseau, *The Collected Writings of Rousseau*, ed. Roger D. Masters and Christopher Kelly, vol. 2 (Hanover, NH: University Press of New England, 1990–2010).

them" (*Letter to Mr. Grimm*, *CW*, 2:85). Later he was to apply a similar claim to readers of the *Second Discourse* and, again, to attacks on *Emile*. In this respect, *Rousseau: Judge of Jean-Jacques* merely brings to the fore an oft repeated complaint.

With this preliminary, it is now possible to turn directly to *Rousseau: Judge of Jean-Jacques*. The enigmatic character of this work is underscored by the fact that near the beginning of each of the three dialogues one or the other of the characters identifies an enigma, or puzzle, in what the other has been saying. The existence of these enigmas highlights the importance of the theme of the difficulty of understanding for this work. I will use these three enigmas to try to show the unity of the work, or at least to indicate how it proceeds.

The Enigma of the Monster

The First Dialogue begins in the midst of things, with the character, "Rousseau's" exclamation: "what incredible things I have just learned! I can't get over it. No, I will never get over it. Just heaven, what an abominable man! How he has hurt me! How I am going to detest him" (*CW*, 1:8). What he has just learned is that "Jean-Jacques," whose books he admires so much, has been proven to be a scoundrel of the worst sort, a criminal, even a monster. "Rousseau" is a reader of a particular sort (and the Frenchman will reveal himself to be a reader of a somewhat different sort). For "Rousseau," the relation between the character of the author and his work is crucial. This is why he is so disoriented by the revelation that "Jean-Jacques" is a proven criminal. To be sure, he concedes that a scoundrel can be a talented writer but denies that he could produce the sort of works that have moved him so much.

The greater significance of this very personal account of reading is indicated later, just before a turning point in the discussion of the First Dialogue, when "Rousseau" gives a sort of autobiographical account of himself. This account gives him a more specific identity as a character and, in some important ways, shows that he is not simply identical to "Jean-Jacques" or to Jean-Jacques Rousseau. This account indicates both his fundamental concerns and the source of his interest in the writings of "Jean-Jacques." He is, of course, a foreigner who has read the books attributed to "Jean-Jacques." He began his life in poverty, becoming successful only to learn that worldly success does not bring happiness. This experience, including disillusionment about "the sweet chimera of friendship" (*CW*, 1:52), led him to a period of despondency. Nevertheless, withdrawal into himself led him to a dependence on religious faith as a source of a happiness that had two components. First, he says, "I tasted an infinite sweetness in the thought that I was not alone." The belief that there is a divine witness to his unhappiness is a consolation. He adds that his belief taught him that his hardships were limited and that he could hope for "the compensations and joys of a better state" (*CW*, 1:52). In short, he believes in a personal God and in His providence.

By itself, however, this faith somehow proves to be insufficient. "Rousseau" found the necessary supplement to it in the books of "Jean-Jacques." He found in "Jean-Jacques" a kindred soul. The fact that such a person exists seems to serve the same function as God understood as a sympathetic witness to undeserved suffering. Earlier he had discussed inhabitants of an ideal world, or "initiates" who recognize each other's writings by means of a "characteristic sign" immediately and intuitively (*CW*, 1:12). This reflects his own experience of reading "Jean-Jacques." "Rousseau" adds later that the writings taught him to find in himself the "enjoyment and happiness that all others seek so far from themselves" (*CW*, 1:53). He does not explain the relation between anticipating a better state and seeking happiness inside oneself. However this may be—and I will return to this question—"Rousseau" found that his reading strengthened his belief "against the derision of free thinkers." He declares, "I was a believer, I have always been one," although he later goes out of his way to insist that he does not believe in miracles (*CW*, 1:76) and is therefore not the most orthodox of believers. In sum, "Rousseau" is interested in "Jean-Jacques" because he finds in his writings a solution to the problem of his own unhappy experience.

"Rousseau's" account of his reading stresses the close personal bond among the author, his works, and his readers. He finds it impossible to believe that this author with whom he identifies so much can be a wicked man. This leads him to insist both that he believes the charges against "Jean-Jacques" and that he knows that the author of the books is no criminal. This causes the Frenchman to say, "as for me, I understand nothing of these enigmas. I beg you to tell me for once your true feeling about him" (*CW*, 1:13). "Rousseau" then offers what he calls "the key to the enigma." To the many crimes committed by Jean-Jacques, he adds the additional one of claiming to be the author of books that were written by someone else. The real author of the books is the good man admired by "Rousseau," while "Jean-Jacques" is a plagiarist on top of his other crimes. Readers who are already confused by the division of Jean-Jacques Rousseau into the characters of "Rousseau" and "Jean-Jacques" are faced with a new division. "Rousseau's" enigma is an attempt to save the books from their association with a proven criminal.

As the dialogue proceeds, "Rousseau" and the Frenchman address the implications of this enigma of the split between the purported author and the real one. The discussion of "Jean-Jacques's" character and his treatment by his accusers leads to a crucial turning point a little over halfway through the discussion.

It becomes clear that, while there is abundant reason to believe that "Jean-Jacques" is the monster he is described to be, he has never been formally convicted of any crime. Indeed, in order to avoid the scandal that public discussion of his crimes would cause, his accusers have been careful to avoid a public confrontation. For "Rousseau," this changes everything. He declares, "oh thank Heaven, I am relieved! You remove a heavy burden from my heart" (*CW*, 1:52). In explaining himself, he develops an elaborate and precise discussion of an implication of Jean-Jacques Rousseau's political thought.

It could seem strange that the lack of a formal conviction would mean so much to "Rousseau," given that he continues to concede the force of the proofs that have been provided of "Jean-Jacques's" wickedness. His position turns on a distinction between these proofs which can produce a persuasion of guilt and genuine evidence that would be necessary to turn this persuasion into conviction in all senses of the term. A part of his insistence comes from examples he gives of trials in which the accused was discovered to be innocent in spite of apparently overwhelming proofs against him. Most importantly he argues, "as long as the accused has not been heard, the proofs that condemn him—however strong they might be, however convincing they might appear—lack the seal that can show them to be so" (*CW*, 1:55). Indeed, he goes so far as to refer to this "great principle" as "the basis and sanction of all justice without which human society would crumble at its foundations." He repeatedly calls this principle "sacred" or "holy" and claims that both the "maintenance of the social order" and the "preservation of the human race" depend on it (*CW*, 1:56).

The force with which "Rousseau" insists upon this "great principle" indicates that its significance extends far beyond the specific instance involving "Jean-Jacques." In effect, "Rousseau" turns his attention to formal requirements of a genuine condemnation. It is no accident that his examples involve the functioning of juries and the need for unanimity. It is the presence of a public hearing at which the accused can answer charges that transforms "proofs" into legal "evidence" and persuasion into conviction. Only the latter is sufficient to convict someone of a crime. The heart of "Rousseau's" argument in the First Dialogue rests on this distinction between "proofs" and "evidence." This distinction can be compared to the distinction that Jean-Jacques Rousseau makes between possession of goods and property in his other writings. In both cases, only the latter is a legal category. Evidence has stood the test of a legal proceeding in which the accused can respond, just as property is bound by the laws establishing it in any community. Rousseau consistently presents the move from the state of nature to civil society as requiring the establishment of accepted legal categories to take the place of purely natural categories which can always be subject to dispute. The issue of transforming a general persuasion into an authentic conviction is hardly the first or last time that Rousseau explores an issue of general importance through an examination of himself and his own situation.[4]

Having established the fundamental point that "Jean-Jacques" has not really been shown to be a monster, "Rousseau" insists that it is necessary to find out what he can say in his defense. At the end of the First Dialogue the two interlocutors agree that "Rousseau" will seek out "Jean-Jacques" and that the Frenchman will read the books he has been unwilling to look at

[4] This is evident in the *Letters Written from the Mountain* where Rousseau argues that his own legal situation is representative of a constitutional crisis in Geneva. At a deeper level, it is also the case in his *Confessions* where the story of his own life dramatizes his principles of human nature. See Christopher Kelly, *Rousseau's Exemplary Life* (Ithaca, NY: Cornell University Press, 1987).

because of the author's reputation. The Second Dialogue consists of "Rousseau's" report about his visit and the Third consists of the Frenchman's report about his reading.

The Enigma of Natural Goodness

The Second Dialogue begins with the announcement of the enigma to be explained in this dialogue. "Rousseau" reports that he has found "Jean-Jacques" to be neither a virtuous man nor "a detestable scoundrel" (*CW*, 1:87). To this the Frenchman replies, "but then what is all this? You are discouraging with your perpetual enigmas." Again, a dialogue begins with a puzzle that requires a key. The Frenchman's understanding is that someone must be either virtuous or vicious and that there is no alternative to the two. The account of "Jean-Jacques" as good, but not virtuous, provides a new moral doctrine that explains "Jean-Jacques's" otherwise admittedly incomprehensible life, which makes him appear to be a monster. This is the reply to the claim that he is a "monster" made repeatedly in the First Dialogue. This dialogue abounds in terms to characterize "Jean-Jacques's" iniquity—terms such as "scoundrel" or "criminal," but "monster" is the crowning insult. A monster is not only wicked but is characterized by a wickedness that has no natural explanation. A thief may be motivated by a natural desire, but "Jean-Jacques's" wickedness defies explanation in natural terms. In the *Encyclopedia*, edited by Diderot and d'Alembert, monsters are described as departures from natural occurrences, either by lacking essential parts or having excessive parts. The example given to illustrate this is an animal born with two heads. Later, in the Third Dialogue, the Frenchman will say of "Jean-Jacques," "if d'Alembert or Diderot took it upon themselves today to affirm that he has two heads, everyone who saw him pass in the street tomorrow would see his two heads very distinctly" (*CW*, 1:233). The moral, rather than physical, monstrosity attributed to "Jean-Jacques" is one explanation of the strange way he lives his life. "Rousseau" provides an alternative one that indicates that a proper understanding of nature provides an explanation of "Jean-Jacques" and implies that his accusers are the monsters. This dialogue then constitutes an explanation and defense of a peculiar way of life that is easily misunderstood. It brings the resemblance of this work to Plato's *Apology* to the fore. Both must account for how the way a particular individual lives his life can (if wrongly interpreted) lead to charges against him.

In the end, this second enigma concerns the concept of natural goodness, a concept which will later prove to be the fundamental principle of "Jean-Jacques's" system (*CW*, 1:213). What "Rousseau" learns from his meeting with "Jean-Jacques," who embodies this principle, the Frenchman later learns from his reading without meeting "Jean-Jacques." Prior to the encounter with either "Jean-Jacques" or his "system," virtue and vice seem to be understood as the frame of reference for morality: anyone who lacks virtue must possess vice. "Jean-Jacques" both represents in his person and demonstrates in his writings an entirely new moral system.

In order to understand "Rousseau's" depiction of "Jean-Jacques" it is useful to keep in mind the account of his own character given in the middle of the First Dialogue. We have seen that he is troubled by the unhappiness of innocent people and that he has looked for answers to this problem in religion and his reading of "Jean-Jacques." It is not surprising that, once he has succeeded in meeting "Jean-Jacques," "Rousseau" questions him about the matters that motivated him in the reading of the books. He gives a list of their topics of conversation, saying "I sounded him out on the nature of the soul, on the existence of God, on the morality of human life, on true happiness, on his thoughts about the doctrine in fashion and its authors, in short on everything that can make known, along with a man's true feelings about the use of this life and its destination, his true principles of conduct" (*CW*, 1:104). Given "Rousseau's" autobiographical account of himself, it is not surprising that the nature of the soul and the existence of God are of particular importance, along with "the use of this life and its destination." These subjects correspond precisely to what he has said about his own most fundamental concerns.

A crucial part of "Rousseau's" account of "Jean-Jacques's" goodness involves a comparison of him with examples of virtue. By far the longest portion of this part consists of a lengthy treatment of "Jean-Jacques" in relation to what can be found in Jesus's Sermon on the Mount in the Book of Matthew. This is particularly important because it relates to the importance "Rousseau" has attributed to his faith in a witness to his innocent suffering and the promise of a reward in a future state. Given that "Rousseau" listed the subject of the existence of God as one of the matters he discussed with "Jean-Jacques," it is not surprising that they would address religious matters, although we have to note that "Rousseau" reports nothing at all about what "Jean-Jacques" told him about the existence of God, one of the topics he explicitly says they discussed. His silence about the results of the conversations on this topic is unsettling.

The confrontation of the goodness of "Jean-Jacques" with the teaching of the Sermon of the Mount begins with a quite specific reference to the Gospel text in the precise context of explaining the nature of goodness. "Rousseau" says about "Jean-Jacques," "he can truly say, in contrast to those people in the Gospel and those in our day, that where his heart is, there too is his treasure" (*CW*, 1:122). This hearkens back to "Rousseau's" autobiographical statement in the First Dialogue in which he says that reading "Jean-Jacques's" books "taught [him] to find within [himself] the enjoyment and happiness that all others seek so far from themselves" (*CW*, 1:53). Now we learn that there is a relation between this teaching and that of Jesus. In Matthew 6, Jesus criticizes a certain type of person saying, "do not store up for yourselves treasures on earth, where moths and vermin destroy, and where thieves break in and steal. But store up for yourselves treasures in heaven, where moths and vermin do not destroy, and where thieves do not break in and steal."[5] Jesus and "Jean-Jacques" both criticize such people who, as "Rousseau" says here, exist both today and at the time of the Gospel. There is, however, a distinction between the two positions. Jesus concludes, "for where your treasure is, there your heart will be also." In short, both Jesus and those being criticized by Him put their hearts where their treasure is. They differ in the location of the treasure. "Jean-Jacques," however, insists that his treasure is in his heart rather than on worldly goods or in heaven. In this respect, even Jesus counts as one of those people of the Gospel with whom "Jean-Jacques" is in contrast. Even Jesus councils looking outside of oneself for the location of the treasure.

Is it not true, one might ask, that "Jean-Jacques" lives with a hopefulness directed toward a reward in heaven, as "Rousseau" had said that he himself did? Shortly before this passage "Rousseau" indicates as much by appealing to providence. Later "Rousseau" returns to this issue with greater precision. First, he says, "Leaping forward sometimes into the future for which he hopes and which he feels is his due, he tries to draw for himself its delights by comparing them to the ills he has been made to suffer unjustly in this world" (*CW*, 1:153). "*Sometimes*," then "Jean-Jacques" finds himself agreeing with Jesus and puts his treasure

[5] Matthew 6:19–20 (King James Version).

in a future reward in heaven, letting his heart follow it there. "Rousseau's" account of "Jean-Jacques" does not stop there, however. He immediately adds, "more often letting his senses collaborate with his fictions, he forms beings in accord with his heart and living with them in a society of which he feels worthy, he soars to the highest heaven" (*CW*, 1:153). In this part of the passage, it appears that, using his heart as his guide, "Jean-Jacques" attains heavenly rewards here and now and that he does so through his own efforts and without the aid of providence. Since "Rousseau" is concerned with "Jean-Jacques's" constant manner of being, rather than more temporary states, it appears necessary to conclude that he most consistently rejects Jesus's exhortation, even though his distress "sometimes" causes him to lapse. These lapses are a part of his character, but they are less revealing of it than is his more constant manner of being.

Immediately after the reference to the Sermon on the Mount, "Rousseau" gives a straightforward and systematic account of "Jean-Jacques's" goodness. He says that "Jean-Jacques" can be considered to be either strong or weak, depending on how one regards him. On the one hand, his will is so constant that it cannot be swayed by "all the powers of the universe" (*CW*, 1:123). So strong is he that it appears that neither man nor the power of God can sway his devotion to his good. On the other hand, although he cannot be diverted, he does often lack the vigor to obtain his goal (see also, *CW*, 1:128). His goodness consists in a certain steadfastness of will or vision, not in a capacity to satisfy his will. His lack of capacity is his weakness; his steadfastness is his strength.

This explains the paradox of goodness, which is neither vice nor virtue. As "Rousseau" says a few pages later, "He would do good, because it would be sweet for him to do so" (*CW*, 1:126). He hastens to add, "but if it were a matter of fighting his fondest desires and breaking his heart to fulfill his duty, would he do that also? I doubt it." Virtue, as opposed to goodness, involves something different from a steadfast devotion to one's good; it requires a willingness and ability to overcome one's fondest desires in the name of duty, even to the point of breaking one's heart. This requires something more than "the voice of nature." "There must be another voice that commands, and nature must remain silent." Although this picture is qualified slightly later, it invites the view that virtue and faith in providence go together, while goodness alone exists independently of that faith. Providence provides the other voice that commands and it also provides the hope for compensation that will allow one to overcome one's fondest desires even when this threatens to break one's heart. Goodness, however, would never allow one to break one's heart by renouncing one's fondest desire. Indeed, it consists in clinging to a fondest desire which is found in one's heart rather than outside of it.

The strongest evidence about whether "Jean-Jacques" pays heed to the sort of commanding voice that demands that one follow one's duty also comes in the confrontation with the Sermon on the Mount. There is one point on which "Rousseau" insists that "Jean-Jacques" does endorse at least one part of the Sermon without equivocation. He says, "I doubt whether another mortal has ever said better and more sincerely to God, *Thy will be done*" (*CW*, 1:152). In the sincerity of his endorsement of the essential teaching of the Lord's Prayer, "Jean-Jacques" is apparently at least the equal of any Christian who has ever lived. One might think that declaring one's submission to divine will would entail obeying all of the commandments that come from the divine voice. Nevertheless, "Rousseau" tacitly or explicitly shows that "Jean-Jacques" is indifferent to every one of the specific commands given in the Sermon. More than once Jesus insists on the importance of pardoning those who have trespassed against one.

"Rousseau" refers to "the great but difficult virtue of pardoning one's enemies," but he denies that "Jean-Jacques" practices this virtue (*CW*, 1:148). Instead, he simply does not think about his enemies unless he is compelled to. "Rousseau" attributes this to the fact that "Jean-Jacques" is "too avid for his own good to have time to think about the ill of another." In other words, it is the strength of his natural goodness rather than his submission to divine will that preserves him against a desire for vengeance, but it also prevents him from overcoming his own desires for the sake of benefiting his neighbor. He does no harm (*CW*, 1:151), not in answer to a commandment from a divine voice, but because he is too lazy to be concerned about others. The most that can be said about "Jean-Jacques" and religious belief is that he intermittently worries about a compensation for his innocent suffering, but his more constant manner of being leaves him indifferent to this and inattentive to any command from a divine voice. Again, his most distinctive characteristic is his avidity for his own good or, to use the language of the *Second Discourse*, he is guided by an ardent interest in his own well-being (*SD*, *CW*, 3:15).[6] The distinctive character of natural goodness requires that neither virtue nor vice distract one from one's own good.

If "Jean-Jacques" ignores the command to pardon those who trespass against him, it is even more true that he fails to ask forgiveness for his own trespasses. This is only partially because his unique attention to his own good keeps him from desiring to harm others. His weakness in the pursuit of his good (and perhaps that pursuit itself) means that he is not altogether immune from vices, including those that entail harm to others.

[6] *SD* refers to the *Second Discourse*, or *Discourse on Inequality* in Jean-Jacques Rousseau, *The Collected Writings of Rousseau*, ed. Roger D. Masters and Christopher Kelly, vol. 3 (Hanover, NH: University Press of New England, 1990–2010).

"Rousseau," to be sure, never characterizes these vices as sins or as trespasses against divine commandments. The desire for independence that characterizes "Jean-Jacques's" goodness turns him away from any sort of dependence upon God's forgiveness. Indeed, natural goodness is as incompatible with any notion of divine forgiveness as it is with any notion of divine command.[7]

In sum, "Rousseau" does insist that he finds support for his own faith in both his reading of and conversations with "Jean-Jacques." He reports "Jean-Jacques's" partial agreement with Jesus's criticism of those who seek their happiness in worldly goods and insists that he embraces the maxim, "Thy will be done." Nevertheless, his account of their meetings clearly indicates that his hero balks at any notion of a divine commandment that would oblige him. Even his hopes for a compensation for his innocent suffering arise only occasionally.[8]

After treating the goodness of "Jean-Jacques" in relation to the Sermon on the Mount, "Rousseau" turns his attention to other forms of excellence, contrasting him to souls "of high calibre" or "true wise men" (*CW*, 1:156) and then to the genuinely virtuous. About the former, he says, "true wise men are cold." Being untouched by passions, they cannot really be considered to be virtuous because they have no need to overcome their passions to do what is right. In this respect they are both like and unlike

---

[7] Jeremiah Alberg has argued that the rejection of God's forgiveness in Christ is the not fully conscious root of the doctrine of natural goodness. See *A Reinterpretation of Rousseau: A Religious System* (New York: Palgrave MacMillan, 2007), 6–9. See pp. 20–37 for Alberg's treatment of *Rousseau: Judge de Jean-Jacques*.

[8] Rousseau also addresses his resistance to commands (specifically ones of human origin) in relation to his goodness in the Sixth Promenade of the *Reveries of the Solitary Walker*. In the Third Promenade he says that his concern for what is good for himself would not allow him to console himself to being damned if that were God's will.

those "phlegmatic and cold people" whose sole passion of amour-propre makes them "hateful, vindictive, implacable." They are like them in being cold, but unlike them in lacking amour-propre. They can be moral out of principle, but they do not deserve credit for it.[9] Like the wise, "Jean-Jacques" is largely immune to amour-propre, but unlike them, apparently, he is warm in the pursuit of his own good in a way that prevents him from following just principles without effort. The genuinely virtuous represent a different type. Like "Jean-Jacques" their passions may be warm, but they know how to govern their hearts and passions (*CW*, 1:157). Moreover, unlike "Rousseau" they do not even require a witness to their suffering. In the end "Rousseau" has explained the enigma of "Jean-Jacques's" failure to be either virtuous or vicious by distinguishing it from a wide variety of other possibilities: Christianity, wisdom, virtue, and vice.

The Enigma of the Conspiracy

The Third Dialogue follows the pattern set by the others by beginning with an enigma. The Frenchman has returned from the country and is ready to give his report on his experience of reading "Jean-Jacques." This time it is "Rousseau" who makes the accusation against the Frenchman who has said that his close reading of "Jean-Jacques's" works have revealed "the irremediable crimes that couldn't have failed to make their Author the most odious of monsters and the horror of the human race" (*CW*, 1:199). To this, "Rousseau" replies, "is it really you talking, and

9 For a treatment of individuals discussed by Rousseau who are characterized by both coldness and attachment to virtue out of principle, see Christopher Kelly, "Rousseau and the Case for and Against Cosmopolitanism," in *In Search of Humanity: Essays in Honor of Clifford Orwin*, ed. Andrea Radasanu (Lanham, MD: Lexington Books, 2015), 331–46.

is it your turn to make enigmas?"[10] The basic enigma of this final dialogue centers on the nature and significance of the persecution undergone by "Jean-Jacques." The first two dialogues are concerned with the misunderstanding of "Jean-Jacques." The third is concerned with the meaning and consequences of this misunderstanding as well as what can be done about it.

In this dialogue the interlocutor, the Frenchman, comes into his own. Earlier he had resisted, but ultimately accepted the positions of "Rousseau." He occasionally makes astute observations, but if one did not look closely at the intelligence of his resistance, one might see him as merely a straw man who exists only to be refuted. Now, when he disagrees on questions such as the nature of the hatred of "Jean-Jacques" and how he and his supporters should behave, his arguments cause shifts in "Rousseau's" positions. It is now "Rousseau" who is exposed as somewhat naïve, for all of his grasp of "Jean-Jacques" and his books.

The effect of the Frenchman's reading has been to teach him that "Jean-Jacques" is a profound and systematic thinker. While "Rousseau" stressed his sense of an immediate personal connection with the author, without denying this, the Frenchman focusses on the effort needed to understand his works. "Rousseau" has explained the goodness of the man, "Jean-Jacques." The Frenchman explains how a close reading of the books teaches the reader about "the great principle that nature made man happy and good, but that society depraves him and makes him miserable" (*CW*, 1:213). Unlike "Rousseau" he arrived at this understanding only by rereading his writings "with more consistency and attention than [he] had" (*CW*, 1:211). In other words, both interlocutors are concerned with the meaning of natural goodness, but they approach it in rather different ways. The

[10] I have altered the translation here because Rousseau uses the same word (*énigmes*) that has earlier been translated as enigma(s).

importance of the Frenchman's reading is that it reflects a possibility available to all readers to come—for example, us—who are unable to imitate "Rousseau" by paying a call on the author in person, who may be prejudiced by our exposure to the author's reputation, and who do not immediately recognize him as a fellow initiate.

The enigma that "Rousseau" finds in the Frenchman's opening statement, that there is nothing surprising in the fact that "Jean-Jacques" is regarded as a monster, leads to an important disagreement between the two. For the Frenchman, the fact that the writings expose the pretentions of powerful members of society such as intellectuals, doctors, kings, the rich, and others makes it natural that these offended parties would strike back. The only surprising thing is that "Jean-Jacques" would have thought that he could write "with impunity" (*CW*, 1:206). To this, "Rousseau" replies that "Jean-Jacques" did, indeed, expect that the powerful would persecute him. He expected "persecution of all kinds" because this is always the fate of those who are bold enough to expose the truth. What he did not expect, and could not have expected, is "dishonor, opprobrium, and defamation" on top of persecution. These elements of his fate have other causes, which "Rousseau" says are "more secret, more fortuitous, more ridiculous" (*CW*, 1:206). While it may be true that the classes of people exposed by "Jean-Jacques" were predisposed to organize against him, the leaders of the conspiracy are motivated by a more personal antipathy that predated "Jean-Jacques's" literary career.

Although *Rousseau: Judge of Jean-Jacques* never abandons "Rousseau's" position, the Frenchman, in fact, comes closer to the one presented in the *First Discourse*. That work does claim to present a universal thesis: that corruption and the influence of the sciences and arts always go hand in hand. Moreover, it presents examples of individuals, like Socrates, the elder Cato, and

Rousseau himself who stand against the powerful prejudice in favor of the sciences and arts. These parts of the argument are meant to apply to all times and places. There are ways, however, in which the contemporary situation is presented as distinctive. First, the invention of the printing press means that dangerous teachings have a greater public impact (*FD*, *CW*, 2:20). More important for our purposes here is a distinction between the way the opponents of the sciences and arts are treated. Rousseau says, "among us, it is true, Socrates would not have drunk the hemlock; but he would have drunk from an even more bitter cup: insulting ridicule and scorn a hundred times worse than death" (*FD*, *CW*, 2:11). This Rousseau seems to be closer to the Frenchman than he is to "Rousseau" who had found the modern proclivity toward dishonor and defamation to be puzzling. The question considered by the Frenchman, however, concerns why ridicule and scorn, in addition to or in place of persecution, are the fate of people who dare to tell the truth in modern times.

When he hears "Rousseau's" claim that the conspiracy against "Jean-Jacques" originated before he became famous and that it has fortuitous and even ridiculous causes, the Frenchman does not object. He does, however, reply that, whatever might be true about the original causes, the effects are quite intelligible. Ultimately his explanation is an account of a transformation of the operation of public opinion in modern times. He says, "among the peculiarities that distinguish our century from all others is the methodical and consistent spirit that has guided public opinion for twenty years" (*CW*, 1:236). To be sure, public opinion has always existed, but in the past, it was arbitrary and subject to random changes as passions varied. Now, however, a "philosophic sect" has organized itself into a body. This sect has formed a somewhat unsteady alliance with the powerful. Together they exercise a much more consistent domination of public opinion than was possible before. They lead opinion through the dissemination of doctrines chosen less for their truth than their usefulness in abetting this project of ruling. In effect, the Frenchman presents what we know as the Enlightenment as an effort of intellectuals to shape previously unruly public opinion to guarantee their own influence.

A part of the drama of the Third Dialogue is shown by the effect of the Frenchman's diagnosis on his friend "Rousseau." While "Rousseau" never explicitly abandons his claim that the plot against "Jean-Jacques" has a personal origin, he ultimately builds on the Frenchman's claims that the plot is connected with a more comprehensive attempt to replace the influence of Christianity with the influence of "the new philosophers." While maintaining the significance of "Jean-Jacques" by saying that the preaching of the new doctrine began with the plot against him, "Rousseau" concedes that it appears to be related to other plots "of which this one is only a piece" (*CW*, 1:241). In the end, both interlocutors agree that nothing less than the political and moral fate of Europe is concerned in the struggle between "Jean-Jacques" and his persecutors. Once again, the most personal of issues are tightly bound with ones of general significance.

We can understand the "conspiracy" this way: modern life is characterized by an attempt to rule the world by making public opinion a more consistent and more easily dominated force. This attempt presents itself as a benevolent effort by intellectuals to make society more rational. The power of "Jean-Jacques's" writings stems from both their exposure of the sinister character of this effort and their presentation of an alternative view of human nature, a view that is not compatible with either the new philosophy or the Christianity that preceded it. Having no refutation for "Jean-Jacques's" systematic understanding and, indeed, having little concern with truth, the "philosophic inquisition" attacks him with the weapons it has ready to hand: ridicule and defamation.

There is a final issue upon which "Rousseau" and the Frenchman begin by disagreeing. From the First Dialogue on, "Rousseau" insists that publicizing "Jean-Jacques's" situation is both a moral obligation and is bound to be effective. He is somewhat optimistic about the possibility of success. "Rousseau" appeals to what he calls the "generally accepted axiom that the truth is uncovered sooner or later" (*CW*, 1:228). Accepting this axiom, he wants it to be discovered sooner rather than later. He believes that a providential history is on "Jean-Jacques's" and justice's side. He presents this as his personal opinion, or a generally held view, without indicating whether "Jean-Jacques" shares it. The Frenchman, however, is more cautious and, it should be said, more sensible. He questions the truth of what is merely "generally accepted." He says, "I would judge that multitudes of characters and events described in history may have no other basis than the invention of those who took it upon themselves to affirm them" (*CW*, 1:230). The fact that the truth comes out in some cases does not allow one to conclude that it always does or will. How do we know how many important historical truths remain buried? The new efforts to exercise control over public opinion might well make these revelations less likely in the future as the Enlightenment rewrites history to suit its own goals.

These, then, are the enigmas of *Rousseau: Judge of Jean-Jacques*. The enigma of "Jean-Jacques's" reputation as a monster leads to a fundamental legal principle of the need to hear an accused speak in his own defense. The enigma of Jean-Jacques's lack of either virtue or vice leads to an account of natural goodness as an alternative to both Christianity and modern anti-Christian doctrines. Finally, the enigma of a conspiracy against Jean-Jacques leads to an account of the high stakes involved in the philosophic attempt to tame the vicissitudes of public opinion.

It would be reassuring to argue that this strange work is now clear. The work itself, however, reminds us to remain cautious about how well we understand it. At the very end of the Third Dialogue, "Rousseau" says, "if we can confer with J. J. about it all, I have no doubt that we could obtain from him much enlightenment that will remain forever extinct, and that we would be surprised ourselves by the ease with which a few words from him would explain enigmas which will otherwise perhaps remain impenetrable through the skillfulness of his enemies" (*CW*, 1:243). There is, however, no sequel showing what these few words might be and we are in no position to pay "Jean-Jacques" a visit. Similarly, in the "History of the Preceding Writing" with which this work closes, Jean-Jacques Rousseau himself refers to "many enigmas" that remain to be solved (*CW*, 1:255). The investigation started by this enigmatic work is in no danger of closing.

8.

TOCQUEVILLE'S REVERIES: ON THE CONDITION OF WOMEN AND THE INFLUENCE OF ROUSSEAU

Christine Dunn Henderson

If it is a truth universally acknowledged, that a single man in possession of a good fortune, must be in want of a wife, then it is also a truth—though perhaps less universally acknowledged—that Jean-Jacques Rousseau exerted a major influence on the thought of Alexis de Tocqueville.[1] Writing to a cousin in 1836, Tocqueville himself attested to Rousseau's impact, saying "there are three men with whom I live a bit every day, Pascal, Montesquieu, and Rousseau."[2] But what, exactly, was the nature of each thinker's influence on Tocqueville? Opinion is far from united here, and scholars have suggested a variety of options. For Montesquieu, attention has been drawn to Tocqueville's general methods and the breadth of his study of American society; the technique of playing off countervailing powers (and tendencies) to secure liberty; the role of mores, and the centrality of liberty as a political end.[3] In Tocqueville's recognition of the human being's

---

[1] (With apologies to) Jane Austen, *Pride and Prejudice*.

[2] Letter to Louis Kergorlay, 10 November 1836 in Alexis de Tocqueville, *Œuvres Complètes*, vol. 13, 1 (Paris: *Éditions Gallimard*, 1977), 418.

[3] The literature here is extensive. See, for example, Raymond Aron, *Main Currents in Sociological Thought*, trans. R. Howard and H. Weaver, 3rd ed., vol. 1 (New Brunswick, NJ: Transaction Publishers, 1999); Jean-Claude Lamberti, *Tocqueville and the Two Democracies*, trans. A. Goldhammer (Cambridge, MA: Harvard University Press, 1989); Lucien Jaume, "In the

body-soul duality, his emphasis on the innate dignity of man's soul, and his awareness of the fundamental ignorance and corresponding unhappy restlessness that characterize the human condition, we find echoes of Pascal.[4]

Rousseau's influence can also be glimpsed in many ways.[5] Tocqueville's eagerness to encounter Native Americans—and his "complete disappointment" at finding only "feeble and depraved" specimens—finds roots partly in Chateaubriand's romantic depictions, but perhaps even more fundamentally in the *Second Discourse*'s portrait of natural man.[6] Similarly, the account of

---

Tradition of Montesquieu: The State-Society Analogy," chap. 4 in *Tocqueville: The Aristocratic Sources of Liberty*, trans. A. Goldhammer (Princeton: Princeton University Press, 2008).

[4] Peter Lawler's *The Restless Mind: Alexis de Tocqueville on the Origin and Perpetuation of Human Liberty* (Lanham, MD: Rowman and Littlefield, 1993) offers the clearest and most complete articulation of the Pascalian Tocqueville. More recent work includes Michael McLendon, "Tocqueville, Jansenism, and the Psychology of Freedom," *American Journal of Political Science* 50 (2006): 664–75; and Aristide Tessitore, "Tocqueville's American Thesis and the New Science of Politics," *American Political Thought* 4, no. 1 (2015): 72–99.

[5] There is a vast literature on this theme, including classics such as George Wilson Pierson, *Tocqueville in America* (Baltimore: The Johns Hopkins University Press, 1996); or Melvin Richter, "Rousseau and Tocqueville on Democratic Legitimacy and Illegitimacy," in *Rousseau and Liberty*, ed. Robert Wolker (Manchester, UK: Manchester University Press, 1995), 70–95. For more contemporary work, see Matthew W. Maguire, "Rousseau and Tocqueville," in *The Rousseauian Mind*, ed. Eve Grace and Christopher Kelly (New York: Routledge: 2019), 437–47. Rousseau's influence can be felt beyond Tocqueville's published works; indeed, the young Tocqueville's reading of "The Profession of Faith of the Savoyard Vicar" from book 4 of the *Emile* is rumored to have led to his loss of faith, a loss which haunted him throughout his life.

[6] See, for example, Barbara Allen, "An Undertow of Race Prejudice in the Current of Democratic Transformation: Tocqueville on the 'Three Races' of North America," in *Tocqueville's Voyages*, ed. Christine Dunn Henderson (Indianapolis: Liberty Fund, 2014), 242–75.

human history with which Tocqueville's *Memoir on Pauperism* opens borrows heavily from Rousseau, and numerous scholars have remarked upon the resemblance between *Democracy in America*'s township government and Rousseau's idealized Geneva.[7] Rousseau's influence also makes itself felt in Tocqueville's recognition of individual freedom as a primary goal, in his awareness of the dangers modernity poses to that freedom, and in his appreciation of the interrelationship of individual and society in the preservation of individual freedom.

These are not, of course, exhaustive lists of how each of the "Big Three" shaped Tocqueville's thought, for my interest is not genealogical. Moreover, any account of Tocqueville's intellectual influences must be balanced against the Frenchman's ambition to differentiate himself from his predecessors by writing something new. Confessing to Kergorlay his desire to create a "*bonne et grande chose*" that would distinguish him and make his reputation, Tocqueville self-consciously aspired to produce an "original" work in *Democracy in America*.[8] This same wish to depart from what had been said before and to blaze a new interpretative path lay at the heart of Tocqueville's refusal to read contemporary works on America during the composition of *Democracy in America*, lest others' ideas influence the development of his own thought.[9]

---

[7] See, for example, Sheldon Wolin, *Tocqueville between Two Worlds* (Princeton: Princeton University Press, 2001), or Christine Dunn Henderson's introduction to *Tocqueville's Memoirs on Pauperism and Other Writings* (South Bend, Indiana: University of Notre Dame Press, 2021).

[8] Arthur Kaledin, *Tocqueville and His America: A Darker Horizon* (New Haven, CT: Yale University Press, 2011), 57, 200.

[9] This may also account for Tocqueville's relative silence about mechanization, transportation, and industry in *Democracy in America*, as these topics lay at the heart of Michel Chevalier's *Lettres sur L'Amérique du Nord*, published between *Democracy in America*'s first and second volumes.

Working from this idea of Tocqueville's efforts to balance his independence and his indebtedness to his intellectual influences, this chapter focuses on Rousseau's influence on Tocqueville, and on one particular aspect of the intersection of the thought of Rousseau and that of Tocqueville: the condition of women. My reason for focusing on women is because it is here that the tension between Tocqueville's own, innovative thought and the ideas of those who helped frame his intellectual universe emerges quite clearly. In particular, I will argue that there is a tension between Tocqueville's portraits of the American girl and of the American wife, and that this tension is due to Rousseau's continued influence on Tocqueville's thought. Tocqueville's account of the American girl and wife asserts that the decision to enter the "domestic cloister"[10] of wifedom and motherhood is one "freely" taken by the young girl, but his own analysis in *Democracy in America* suggests otherwise. By examining the condition of girls and women within the context of *Democracy in America*'s broader analyses of the forces at work in democratic society—in particular, within the context of tyrannical majoritarianism—we are able to see that the girl's nominally free choice is not an example of free choice, individual sacrifice for the common good. Nor should it be read as a microcosm of the healthy democratic polity. Rather, within the context of majoritarian mores supporting the gendered division of labor, the young girl's decision to self-cloister must be seen either as coerced capitulation to dominant mores, or as an example of the internalization of those repressive norms and consequent (mal)adaptive preference formation.

Arguing that the young girl's preferences have been determined by the circumscribed set of majority-endorsed

[10] "Cloister" is Tocqueville's own language of choice for the woman's place in the family.

options before her is not playing fast and loose with Tocqueville's ideas, for it is precisely this type of adaptive behaviour that lies at the heart of his analysis of the tyranny of the majority over thought and of which he is aware in several different case studies within *Democracy in America*. Yet, Tocqueville is unable to acknowledge this same phenomenon at work with girls/women. Why is this the case? Some have argued that this reflects Tocqueville's own (lapsed) Catholic sensibilities, while others find in it reflections of Tocqueville's complicated feelings about women themselves or about democratic society in general.[11] In contrast with these possibilities, this chapter will suggest that Tocqueville's inability to see the tyrannical majoritarianism shaping the young girl's "choice" to assume the roles of wife and mother within the domestic cloister is due to the lingering influence of Rousseau and that Tocqueville's dependence on a particular version of the Rousseauian lens blinds him to applications of his own theories that would have otherwise been evident to him. While Tocqueville is too close a follower of Rousseau in some senses, I would suggest that, paradoxically, his ambition to offer something analytically new also prevented him from following Rousseau closely enough in other senses. Had Tocqueville been a closer reader of Rousseau, he might have recognized that Rousseau's sustained treatments of particular

[11] Cheryl Welch, for example, interprets Tocqueville's endorsement of separate spheres as part of a "larger web of cultural apprehension," and finds that his inability to sympathize with the plight of women reflects his "particular fears." See Cheryl Welch, *De Tocqueville* (Oxford: Oxford University Press, 2001), 191. Others, such as Laura Janara and Sheldon Wolin, emphasize the influence of the French context on Tocqueville's thinking about American women. Laura Janara, *Democracy Growing Up: Authority, Autonomy, and Passion in Tocqueville's "Democracy in America"* (Albany: State University of New York Press, 2002); Wolin, *Tocqueville.*

women—namely, Sophie and Julie—may offer lessons that are in tension with his discussions of women more generally.

Although this chapter's assertion is that Tocqueville's portrait of the American woman is shaped by his reading of Rousseau, it is the distance between Rousseau and Tocqueville on the woman question that first strikes the reader of *Democracy in America*. In the *Emile*, Rousseau suggests that fundamental differences between the sexes render impossible an evaluative comparison of them, and that "a perfect woman and a perfect man ought not to resemble each other in mind any more than in looks" (*E*, 358).[12] Here, Rousseau speaks of the two sexes within society, already removed from the state of nature in which men and women are equal in significant ways. Like the *Second Discourse*, in which once-insignificant physical differences assume greater moral and political importance over the course of human development, book five of the *Emile* notes that "the physical leads us unawares to the moral" (*E*, 360). The fact that biology links women more directly—and for more extended periods—to the consequences of sex precipitates a gradual modification of the nature of women,[13] rendering them more dependent, first on particular men and eventually on public opinion more generally (*E*, 364).

Rousseau tells his reader that women in society "love adornment," that they desire to appear pleasing, and that they crave the good opinions of those around them (*E*, 365). Following from the notion that within society the natural condition of women is dependence (*E*, 370), Rousseau advocates

[12] *E*, cited by page number, will refer to: Jean-Jacques Rousseau, *Emile: or, On education*, ed. and trans. by Allan Bloom (New York: Basic Books, 1979).

[13] For Rousseau, human nature—both male and female—is essentially protean.

an education for women that emphasizes other-directedness and that, in this sense, stands at odds with Emile's education in independence. If "opinion is the grave of virtue among men" because it destroys their independence and replaces *amour de soi-même* with amour-propre, opinion is virtue's "throne among women" (*E*, 365). A girl's education is a sheltered one that acknowledges and reinforces feminine docility and the importance of conformity to prevailing norms. Girls are taught to avoid social sanction by always appearing modest, chaste, and whatever other qualities have been deemed socially desirable. Here, Rousseau emphasized the importance of habituating the girl to "subjection" (*E*, 370), first to mothers, then to societal mores, and ultimately—though with reservations—to husbands.

Beyond social acceptance and conformity, the education of "civilized" woman (as opposed to natural woman) is intended to prepare her for her roles as mother and as helpmate. As Rousseau notes, "the whole education of women ought to relate to men. To please men, to be useful to them, to make herself loved and honoured by them, to raise them when young, to care for them when grown, to counsel them, to make their lives agreeable and sweet—these are the duties of women" (*E*, 365). Rousseau underscores the importance of feminine piety and the role of mothers in instilling corrective religious mores in the next generation. Similarly, he emphasizes both in *Emile* and in the *Letter to D'Alembert* that women must be sheltered from various aspects of public life in order to preserve their virtuous character which, via the roles of wife and mother, is essential to the preservation of virtue in society more generally. Indeed, it is for these reasons that Rousseau speaks approvingly of the Spartan "cloistering" of women within the domestic sphere (*E*, 366).

In contrast with Rousseau's young women, who are brought up under strict maternal guidance and taught to value modesty and conformity to convention, the American girls observed by Tocqueville follow different paths. Unlike Rousseau's young girls—or their European counterparts more generally—the American girl enjoys considerable freedom from an early age; according to Tocqueville, before she has fully left childhood, "already she thinks by herself, speaks freely, and acts alone" (*DA*, 1042).[14] Tocqueville attributes the freedom enjoyed by young girls to the effects of Protestantism and to the ethos of democratic society, noting that "nowhere is the young girl more quickly or more completely left to herself" than in America (*DA*, 1042). Rather than sheltering and protecting their daughters, American parents deliberately expose their daughters to the world as it is, with its vices and dangers. The aim of this early education is to cultivate the reason, calm, and judgment necessary for the American girl to make wise use of her liberty. Her judging and self-regulating abilities are strengthened through use, and the sphere of her independence expands as she matures. In Tocqueville's view, the American girl's free upbringing (i.e., the gradual expansion of her freedom as her experience grows) develops the strength and confidence that prevent her from being overwhelmed or swept away by the tumult of democratic society. Tocqueville notes, "she enjoys all permitted pleasures without abandoning herself to any one of them, and her reason never relinquishes the reins, although it often seems to let them hang loosely" (*DA*, 1043).

The practical education received by the American girl seems to differ in no significant way from the education appropriate to young American men. The explanation for this is that although Tocqueville does concede physical difference between the sexes,

---

[14] *DA*, cited by page number, will refer to: Alexis de Tocqueville, *Democracy in America*, ed. Eduardo Nolla, trans. James T. Schleifer (Indianapolis: Liberty Fund, 2010).

he does not treat these differences as indicative of intellectual or temperamental inequalities, nor does he utilize them to legitimize legal and institutional hierarchies. Instead, *Democracy in America*'s descriptions of American girls emphasize their intellectual and moral equality (*DA*, 1063, 1065)—indeed, their superiority—to their male counterparts.[15] Similarly, Tocqueville repeatedly describes American girls in masculinized terms: intrepid, courageous, honest, firm, "possessing male reason and an entirely male energy" (*DA*, 1064).

With independence, activity, and self-regulation as the American girl's most striking characteristics, Tocqueville's descriptions of her youthful freedom and self-command prepare the reader to anticipate the payoff to her practical education in the ways of the world: a future in which the adult female would fully participate in democratic public life[16] as an equal, artfully navigating democratic life's shoals so that feminine virtue and human freedom remain intact. Yet, this is famously not the case, for a different future awaits the girl upon reaching adulthood, and her situation undergoes a dramatic change with marriage. Her early freedom vanishes completely, and her life is spent "cloistered" in her husband's home.[17] As a wife, she follows the model endorsed by Rousseau, devoting herself to the moral/religious education of the next generation of democratic citizens and providing a haven of stability amidst democratic flux.

Within *Democracy in America*'s chapters devoted to American girls, to women, and to marriage, Tocqueville writes approvingly of the feminine cloistering within the domestic

---

[15] See *DA* 1067, note m: "Say clearly somewhere that the women seem to me very superior to the men in America."

[16] Socially, and perhaps even politically.

[17] Note the echo of Rousseau's approval of the treatment of Spartan women. See p. 197, above.

sphere, emphasizing that this removal from public life in the name of inculcating the next generation with salutary mores is good and that the girl's choice to undertake this radical shift in her life is a free one. Yet the contrast between his sketches of the American girl and the American wife must give any attentive reader pause. Within a few years, the vigorous and independent—indeed, the entrepreneurial—girl has been transformed into a wan and weakened spectre of her younger self, whose features are described as "altered" and "austere" (*DA*, 1051). The price of entering the conjugal cloister appears to have been the girl's very life force, which Tocqueville suggests has drained from her and has been transmitted to her offspring. Observing an American wife on the frontier, he comments, "her children crowd around her; they are full of health, excitement, and energy. . . To see their strength and her weakness, you would say she has exhausted herself by giving them life" (*DA*, 1289–90). The quasi-parasitic image Tocqueville summons explains the mother's melancholic expression, in that her sadness is surely a recognition of the cost she has borne for securing the next generation of democratic citizens.[18]

Other portions of *Democracy in America* introduce further complications to Tocqueville's explicit approval of the girl's choice to self-cloister and his assertions of the freedom with which that choice is made. It is on the basis of these other portions of *Democracy in America* that a Tocquevillian argument can be developed asserting that the girl's choice to retire from

---

[18] Melancholy is one half of the mother's mixed emotions. Tocqueville describes her looks as "full of joy and melancholy," concluding that she does not regret motherhood's costs. Could it be, however, that Tocqueville is projecting in order to justify his own theory; more importantly still, are the mother's emotions authentic, or are they responses which have been conditioned by her environment? See pp. 204–208, below.

public life is neither good nor free. In particular, Tocqueville's discussions of the industrial division of labor and of individualism suggest that female withdrawal into a separate sphere is beneficial neither for the individual girl nor for society. Similarly, *Democracy in America*'s analysis of tyranny of the majority supports the conclusion that the American girl's choice is not freely made in any robust sense.

In his endorsement of the American woman's decision to retire from public life and to focus solely on domestic matters such as moral education, Tocqueville associates this arrangement with efficiency and progress. Comparing the domestic to the industrial, he observes that "the Americans applied to the two sexes the great principle of political economy that dominates industry today. They carefully divided the functions of the man and the woman, in order that the great work of society was better accomplished" (*DA*, 1063). Yet, this apparent support for the American domestic division of labor is undermined by *Democracy in America*'s explicit treatment of the industrial division of labor, which Tocqueville criticizes as harmful not simply to the individual worker, but to society more generally. The developed division of labor, Tocqueville argues, contracts the worker's spirit and intellect, causing him to become "weaker, more limited, and more dependent" (*DA*, 982). In contrast to the ideal of the self-governing citizen of the New England township, the division of labor transforms the industrial worker into a "brute" who "seems born only to obey" (*DA*, 983). At its furthest extension, Tocqueville envisions the division of labor as creating class divisions of industrialists who are permanent commanders and workers who are permanent followers. Contemplating this future, he asks "what is this, if not aristocracy?" (*DA*, 983). In its opposition to equality, which *Democracy in America* repeatedly casts as providential and just, Tocqueville seems to be telling us that the division of labor is unnatural and perhaps even unjust. Thus, it would appear that the division of labor should be avoided at all costs, and it is difficult to imagine why the domestic division of labor would be exempted from Tocqueville's critiques of the division of labor more generally. Indeed, Tocqueville offers no indications that the division of labor itself yields categorically different consequences in the domestic sphere, or that it is beneficial—rather than demeaning—to the various specialized workers.

If Tocqueville's critiques of the industrialized division of labor raise questions about its domestic variant, a similar difficulty arises when Tocqueville's endorsement of the American woman's withdrawal from public life is scrutinized more closely. Broadly speaking, *Democracy in America* endorses engagement—political and civil engagement, local town life, etc. Such forms of communal activity strengthen "public virtues" by connecting citizens to each other, by instilling in them the sense of shared purposes, and by strengthening respect for law and for individual rights. By empowering and connecting individuals, engagement endeavors to recreate democratic variants of the energy and strength that had helped preserve freedom and greatness in previous ages. Isolation, by contrast, is generally viewed by Tocqueville as dangerous to both the individual and society. Tocqueville's analysis of individualism, a vice distinctive to democratic ages, allows us to see this most clearly.

Unlike the perennial vice of egoism, individualism is unique to democratic ages and owes its genesis to the elevation of individual reason that is a direct consequence of the breakdown of aristocratic hierarchies. Tocquevillian individualism is rational rather than passionate; it is described as a "peaceful and considered sentiment" that teaches the democratic individual to care more for what belongs to him than for the goods of common life. In particular, the individualist values material well-being and connection to the "small society" of family and friends, seeking to pursue these things exclusively by removing himself from public life and withdrawing entirely into the private sphere (*DA*, 882). Tocqueville is critical of the effects of this withdrawal on society as well as the individual. Politically, the individual's withdrawal from public life is disastrous, because it creates a public void into which the softly despotic government easily steps. Personally, the thoroughgoing individualist can be dangerously selfish, characterized by Tocqueville as coarse, with an "impoverished" soul.[19]

Extrapolating from Tocqueville's praise of various forms of engagement and his condemnation of the individualist's withdrawal from public life, it seems safe to assume that withdrawal in general should be regarded with skepticism in the Tocquevillian universe. Yet puzzlingly, the American woman's choice to follow the individualist's path and to withdraw into the private circle is treated as praiseworthy. Both the individualist and the woman are said to exercise "cold" judgment in deciding to abandon the public sphere, but Tocqueville assesses these self-removals differently, prompting us to wonder why the woman's withdrawal is beatified while the individualist's is condemned.[20]

Thus far, we have found in Tocqueville's discussions of the economic division of labor and individualism the resources to call into question his claims that American domestic arrangements are good, insofar as they are dependent upon the sexual division

---

[19] Or in the words of Jack Turner, "a self-deluded moral failure." *Awakening to Race: Individualism and Social Consciousness in America* (Chicago: University of Chicago Press, 2012), 16.

[20] Lisa Pace Vetter, "Tocqueville's American Woman and 'The True Conception of Democratic Progress'" in *Feminist Interpretations of Alexis de Tocqueville*, ed. Jill Locke and Eileen Hunt Botting (University Park: The Pennsylvania State University Press, 2009), 157–58.

of labor and upon the same type of removal from the public sphere that Tocqueville associates with dangerous individualism. Tocqueville had further claimed that the young girl's decision to remove herself from public life was also a choice freely made, yet Tocquevillian resources can be marshalled to call into question this claim as well.

When describing the transition from young girl to wife, Tocqueville is at pains to assert that the girl's decision to "put herself under the yoke" by entering into the confines of marriage is a free one (*DA*, 1065) for which her early independence has prepared her. Immediately following this assertion, however, Tocqueville calls into question the robustness of this choice by hinting at the narrowed range of socially acceptable options before the young girl. Noting that "the most virtuous" women (i.e., those who chose traditional married life) characterized their sacrifice of freedom as a glorious self-sacrifice for the greater good, Tocqueville adds that "the others [women] kept silent" (*DA*, 1065). Thus, he hints at the possibility that some women would have chosen not to sequester themselves in the home and that those women felt free neither to express that preference nor to act on it. Within the chapters on girls and women, Tocqueville offers no further insight into these would-be dissenters and the reasons for their silence. To better understand the silence of these women who would prefer to make other life choices, we should examine the dynamics by which social conformity is created and maintained. Here, *Democracy in America*'s discussions of the tyranny of the majority offer valuable insights and cast a more sinister light upon the freedom of the girl's choice to follow the path of wifedom/motherhood, as well as upon the silence of "the others."

Indeed, the very language Tocqueville deploys in describing the American girl's decision to follow socially accepted feminine roles echoes volume one's discussions of tyrannical majoritarianism. There, Tocqueville emphasizes that individuals are free to dissent while majority opinion is undecided, but once consensus on a given question emerges, difference of opinion is no longer tolerated and "friends as well as enemies then seem to climb on board together" (*DA*, 418). As soon as majority opinion has solidified, social sanction of heterodox points of view is absolute, reaching across all areas of public and private life. The social sanction suffered by the dissenter as said to be "a fate worse than death," for the non-conformist finds herself "a stranger among us" (*DA*, 418). *Democracy in America* traces how fear of this sanction stifles the very idea of dissent or nonconformist behaviour before it can be fully formed,[21] as well as how the individual comes to internalize majoritarian perspectives by exercising free choice, but only within the narrowed range of permitted options. Characterized by Tocqueville as "tyranny that acts upon the very soul," this type of self-censorship and adaptive preference behaviour is particularly dangerous, for it is a type of unfreedom that is entirely consistent with the external forms and processes of democratic liberty; as such, it shares important characteristics with the two democratic tyrannies—tyranny of the majority (over thought) and soft despotism—about which Tocqueville warns.

When read via the lens provided by Tocqueville's discussions of the tyranny of the majority, the coerced aspects of the young girl's "choice" come through quite clearly. By Tocqueville's own descriptions, it is "unanimous consent" and "inexorable public opinion" that require the girl to remain in the domestic cloister and to devote herself exclusively to her husband and children; any

[21] In Timur Kuran's words, how "the unthinkable" becomes "the unthought." See Timur Kuran, "The Unthinkable and the Unthought," in *Rationality and Society* 5, no. 4 (October 1993): 473–505.

girl flouting these norms recognizes that she would be "immediately endangering her tranquillity, her honor, and even her social existence" (*DA*, 1049). The girl is free, as Tocqueville notes, to become the wife of any man (*DA*, 1054), but she is clearly not free to become the wife of no man at all.

Tocqueville's discussions of tyranny of the majority allow us to see how repressive norms enforce conformity, not only through the social sanctioning of dissenters, but also even more effectively and lastingly, through the internalization of those norms by the would-be dissenting individual herself. Beyond the discussions of girls and women, *Democracy in America* includes sketches of each of these modes of oppression at work. Describing the manner in which individuals silence themselves because they fear the consequences of opposing majority option, Tocqueville recounts a conversation with a Pennsylvania man, in which he asked the Pennsylvanian why freed Blacks remain excluded from the rights and privileges of full democratic citizenship, despite the removal of legal barriers to their inclusion.[22] The Pennsylvanian explains to Tocqueville that although rights had been granted to Blacks, segregationist mores remain dominant in the North and prevent the enforcement of equal rights. Queried about why white magistrates do not enforce the laws protecting Blacks' rights, the Pennsylvanian concedes that the magistrates "do not feel they have the strength" to oppose decided majority will. Individuals who oppose majority points of view find neither remedy nor support, leading Tocqueville to conclude that "however iniquitous or unreasonable the measure that strikes you may be, you must therefore submit to it" (*DA*, 574).[23] If members of the

[22] Slaves' self-understandings are also shaped by dominant beliefs, though here, the dominance is juridical and political, if not always numerical.

[23] That this conversation occurs in a Quaker context—i.e., in a part of American society well-known for its emphasis on the fundamental equality of

empowered community, such as whites in the magistrate example, feel unable to voice their dissent and compelled to conform to the majority's position, members of disempowered communities would be even less able to resist. It is not difficult to imagine how women who might prefer lives other than the majority-sanctioned roles of wife and mother would feel compelled to conform.

Through Tocqueville's depiction of the Black slaves, we also glimpse how the majority's point of view comes to be internalized by others and how that internalization produces a conformity that is voluntary insofar as it is willingly chosen but whose robustness is questionable. Commenting upon the tragic condition of Black slaves, Tocqueville observes,

> Plunged into this abyss of evils, the Negro scarcely feels his misfortune;...the practice of servitude has given him the thoughts and ambition of a slave; he admires his tyrants even more than he hates them, and finds his joy and his pride in servile imitation of those who oppress him. His intelligence has fallen to the level of his soul. (*DA*, 517)

Slavery's physical violence, then, is accompanied by a psychological violence, and Tocqueville's description indicates that the slave has internalized the perspectives and values of the dominant group, eventually transforming into what the majority believes the slave to be. Because the experience of oppression has left the slave with only "the thoughts and ambition of a slave," we must wonder whether the experience of slavery has been so psychologically distortive that any of the slave's expressed

---

all humans and for its staunch opposition to slavery—intensifies Tocqueville's comments about the magistrate's fear of speaking against the dominant Anglo-American majority.

preferences should be viewed more skeptically, as more likely to have been framed and determined by the oppressive context, and less likely to be indicative of his or her own true interests. The girl's choice to enter the marital cloister should be viewed with similar skepticism, and we must ask whether the choice is freely made in any robust sense, or whether it is better understood as her unconscious adaptation to the limited range of options available to her.

Within *Democracy in America*'s discussions of the tyranny of the majority over thought and in other passages within the text, then, Tocqueville demonstrates his awareness of oppression's subtler sides and of manners in which repressive norms can deter not simply the expression but also the formation of heterodox views. Yet, when it comes to applying this understanding of oppression's nuances to the case of young women, Tocqueville is unable to see the conclusion to which his own analyses point, just as he is unable to apply his critiques of individualism and of the industrial division of labor to the domestic context. In all of these cases, we must ask what accounts for this almost willful blindness on the Frenchman's part?

Let me suggest that the answer lies in Tocqueville's sources. Hugh Brogan's comment "if Tocqueville and Beaumont ever had a serious conversation with an American woman, no record of it survives," is correct, for although Tocqueville's notebooks do contain accounts of conversations with American matrons, those exchanges appear to have been minimal and only at the most superficial of levels.[24] By contrast, Tocqueville and Beaumont did spend considerable time in the company of and in conversation with young women. Tocqueville's accounts of the free and self-governing American girl thus appear to derive from his own

[24] Hugh Brogan, *Alexis de Tocqueville: A Life* (New Haven, CT: Yale University Press, 2006), 158.

experiences with young women in the United States and to reflect what he had observed around him. His discussions of the choices and life of the married woman, however, are more tenuously rooted in first-hand research, for Tocqueville spent little to no time in substantive conversation with American matrons. Lacking direct materials for analyzing the condition of American women, Tocqueville reverts to his influences, offering an account of the American wife that diverges sharply from his earlier depiction of the American girl's energetic independence and that more closely resembles the Rousseauian model.

It is this reliance on the Rousseauian account, I would suggest, that blinds Tocqueville to the subtler unfreedoms to which American women are subjected and to which his own analysis in *Democracy in America* points. In his discussions of relations between the sexes, Tocqueville's analytic point of departure is freedom and equality of both sexes, and he is aware of power's softer faces. Rather than seeing how the girl might be victim to these forces and how her nominally free choice might nonetheless be subject to constraints imposed by the majority and internalized by the girl herself, however, he relies upon a framework derived from book 5 of the *Emile* which emphasizes the civic benefits secured by traditional roles and by the sexual division of labor. This leads him to ignore more subtle forms of social coercion suggested within his own account of American womanhood.

Certainly, some scholars might spring to Rousseau's defense, pointing out that the beginning of book 5 of the *Emile* is far from Rousseau's only discussion of women. These defenders might draw attention to the *Julie*, in which Julie's fate points to quite a different assessment of the costs to the individual of conformity to majority opinion and of the sexual division of labor.[25] Similarly, within the *Emile*, these defenders might point to the contrast between the general discussion of women and Sophie's own education, which emphasizes her self-command, her oblique control of Emile, and the cultivation of independent judgment about when majoritarian mores should be followed—and when they should not.[26]

In response to these defenders, I am prepared to concede that had Tocqueville been a better student and closer reader of Rousseau, he would have taken away different lessons about the nature and proper roles of women, and that these might have transformed his *Democracy in America* discussions, making him more aware of the tensions in his depictions of girls and women, and allowing him to recognize the unfreedoms to which his own analyses point. But in his desire to write something new, something different, Tocqueville rejected rereading and consulting with his sources, including those (like Rousseau) that had most fundamentally shaped his thinking. And so, because of this, we find within *Democracy in America* a shell of Rousseau's thinking on women, rather than its full substance.

---

[25] Susan Moller Okin observes that "what we learn from the denouements of the stories of Rousseau's ideal women"—i.e., the fates of both Sophie and Julie—"is that his prescription for women was an impossible one, even within the confines of his own thought and writing." "Rousseau's Natural Woman," *The Journal of Politics* 41, no. 2 (May 1979): 393–416.

[26] For a more complete account of Sophie as a critical response to book 5's presentation of "woman" in general, see Denise Schaeffer, *Rousseau on Education, Freedom, and Judgment* (University Park: The Pennsylvania State University Press, 2014), 134–57.

INDEX